WHY CAN'T A
❊ MAN ❊
BE MORE LIKE A
❧ WOMAN? ❧

WHY CAN'T A ❀ MAN ❀ BE MORE LIKE A ❀ WOMAN? ❀

Sandra L. Beckwith

KENSINGTON BOOKS

KENSINGTON BOOKS are published by

Kensington Publishing Corp.
850 Third Avenue
New York, NY 10022

First Printing: May, 1995
ISBN: 0-8217-4926-9

Printed in the United States of America

To my husband, Bill Assimon,
whose love, insight, and understanding
helped make this book possible.

❧ Acknowledgments ❧

Leading the list of people I'd like to thank is Jane Grant Tougas, a creative and funny friend who has helped this project tremendously with her editing, but also by continuously faxing me relevant clippings from magazines and newspapers, anecdotal material from friends (and strangers!), and information on experts to interview. I owe her big time.

I also want to thank my visionary editor, Beth Lieberman, who pursued this project with enthusiasm and my agent, David Black, who grasped its potential immediately, in spite of his gender. Thanks, too, to my family, particularly my husband, Bill Assimon, who has supported *The Do(o)little Report* and this book from the beginning; my parents, Steve and Liz Beckwith, for not disowning me; my siblings, Cathy Hughes, Diane Shephard, and Debby, Gary, Steve, and Rick Beckwith for their steady encouragement; and my daughters, Jessica and Alexandra Assimon, who have been very patient with Mommy's deadlines.

In addition, I want to acknowledge the contributions of friends Steve Crane, Bert and Ed Garman, Sue Hertz, Jay Johnson, Marcia Layton, Charlotte Libov, Jan Regan, Shelley Page, Sue Sampson, Jill Stewart, Lee Tougas, and Sandy Ursini, along with my assistant, Janet VanDenHandel. Thanks, too, to the experts who agreed to interviews for this book and the introspective male authors of the "Women want to know" columns.

I must also thank the staff members of the Fairport, New York, post office, who have handled with skill and patience the thousands of pieces of mail generated by my national television appearances.

Finally, my really, really sincere thanks go to the men of America who inspired this book. Fellows, you crack me up! Please don't stop being "you."

✌ Contents ✌

✌

Foreword, by John Gray, Ph.D.   xiii

Introduction   1

1:   The Dawn of the Wheel   5

"Honey, wasn't that our turn?" Why men don't ask for directions

The garage as a sacred place

"I'll wait for you in the car!"

2:   Men Make Fire   15

Why men barbecue

The four major male food groups

What a gas!

3:   From Bearskin to Polyester   27

Women shop, men get

What is it with men and stereos? by Lee Tougas

Men's clothing should be labeled with expiration dates

The crowning glory: Why men wear baseball caps

4: Tribal Rituals   43

Distant replay: Why men set the VCR to tape games they attend

Channel surfing USA by Steve Crane

Bubba, Bonzo, and Biff: Why men give each other nicknames

Why men love sports by Bill Assimon

That magical instrument, the air guitar

Why do men fish? by Steve Crane

5: Mating Rituals   59

Why don't they call after the first date?

Want to see my dentures? Why older men date younger women

For better or for worse: Why men marry

6: There's No Cave like Home   71

"Where are my car keys?" Why men can't find things that are right under their noses

Male time dysfunction, or why it takes two weeks to change a lightbulb by Tom Powell

Do sick men make women sick?

7: Reproducing the Species   83

Why men have children

Men in labor

It's parenting, *not* babysitting!

8: Beyond the Stone Tablet   100

Male Answering Syndrome: The cause, the cure

"Well, why didn't you ask?"

Male support groups: The solution to women's problems?

"What did you mean by that?*"*

The passive-aggressive male and you

9: Intelligence   122

Men and common sense

Men who can do more than one thing at a time

Adult education for men

*Nyuk, nyuk, nyuk! Men explain their attraction to
    The Three Stooges*

ADD in adult males: Arrested Development Disorder

10: Is Evolution Possible?   134

ᴄ Foreword ᴠ

by John Gray, Ph.D.

I have subscribed to Sandra Beckwith's humorous newsletter about men, *The Do(o)little Report,* since the first issue. The unique style I've enjoyed in that publication is reflected in this lighthearted book addressing women's most commonly asked questions about male behavior.

Sandra's approach is unique in that she encourages women to accept men *as they are,* without changing them. This is so important to the health of a relationship. Men and women *are* different and always will be. The theory behind this book is that if you understand why a man does what he does, or says what he says, you'll be more tolerant and less frustrated in your relationship. I agree wholeheartedly.

One reason I like *Why Can't a Man Be More Like a Woman?* is that the author doesn't pretend to have all the answers. Instead, she turns to men for explanations about their behavior and attitudes on issues ranging from dating to parenting to sports. When Sandra shares this information with readers, she also explains how they can cope with—not modify—male behavior that frustrates them.

The result is therapeutic. While women learn they are not alone as they struggle with a particular male "quirk," they also laugh because of the lighthearted way in which the information is presented. Whether the topic is the age-old issue about asking for directions when lost, or Sandra's theory that men's clothing should be labeled with expiration dates, she presents information and advice in a uniquely offbeat way that makes readers chuckle.

And laughter is so important. In my workshops, books, and videotapes, I encourage couples to maintain a sense of humor as they work through their problems or differences. *Why Can't a Man Be More Like a Woman?* is one tool they can use to do that. It should be read by both genders. Men will learn what women are interested in while discovering more about themselves. Women will appreciate the lift they receive as they struggle to cope with the pressures of today's hectic lifestyles.

This book is written with a distinctly female sense of humor best described as a cross between *Saturday Night Live* and Deborah Tannen's bestselling *You Just Don't Understand!* It's refreshing to see so much useful material presented in such a fun way. I will certainly recommend it to the couples I work with as one more tool they can use to understand each other better.

John Gray, Ph.D.

Author of *Men Are from Mars,
Women Are from Venus*
and *What Your Mother Couldn't Tell You
and Your Father Didn't Know*

Why Can't a
❈ MAN ❈
Be More Like a
❧ WOMAN? ❧

❧ Introduction ❧

❧❧❧

Not long ago, I was downright befuddled by my husband's behavior. I couldn't understand his obsession with sports. Or how he could walk around a puddle on the floor, then claim he didn't clean it up because he didn't see it. And communication? It was like hosting a foreign exchange student.

Everyone knows that men and women are different, but I didn't realize the extent of the differences—and the problems they can cause in relationships—until my own frustrations forced me to tune in a little more closely to conversations among other women. I listened to the commentary among neighbors and friends. I eavesdropped on women in supermarkets and restaurants. I studied the dialogue of sitcoms. A common denominator in all these conversations was confusion caused by male behavior.

Get a group of women together and they'll talk about their children, their jobs, even what they use to remove that waxy yellow build-up on their kitchen floors. And eventually, they will always talk about what frustrates them in their relationships with men. Not because they like to whine and complain but rather because they need each other for information and support.

Running through all this casual group therapy is a strong need to understand what makes men so different from women. There are explanations, of course. One popular Darwinian theory is that differences result from "survival of the fittest" evolution. Traditional male-female roles have required different skills—for example, women with shopping expertise have survived to feed and clothe families. At the same time, men with an ability to create fire—and hence barbecue—have become prized mates in the evolutionary struggle.

But this suggests that women have influenced this process when selecting an appropriate mate for procreation. Doesn't that seem like a ridiculous idea—would women actually select a man for his ability to play *air guitar?*

Another theory suggests men are from another planet. While I suspect that one's a little closer to the truth, I've rejected both theories and done my own research. I needed to know what could possibly explain why men can barbecue, but not cook; why they wear out remote control batteries on a weekly basis; why they think the Three Stooges are funny.

It was the male assumption that women have an extra gene to help them find something right under the male nose that set off a lightbulb in my head. Why, that's right! It's not that women have an extra gene—it's that men and women have *different* genes!

I knew I was right when I stumbled across the research of Jane Gitschier, Ph.D., a geneticist at the University of California, San Francisco. Although Gitschier knew she had to present her discovery as a joke (given the male tendency to avoid self-examination or, to use the Latin term, *introspectus vacuii*), she confirmed what most women already know: The Y ("Why?") chromosome found only in men is coded for gadgetry, channel flipping, throwing and catching, addiction to death and destruction movies, and so on (see accompanying diagram).

It's shocking, maybe a little frightening. But the truth about why a man can't be more like a woman has been ignored because it challenges all theories about the origin of the species. Is there a cover-up among leaders of the scientific community? Are they collaborating with psychologists and sociologists on this one?

I'm not sure.

The evidence isn't conclusive yet, but so far, my research leads

MAP OF THE HUMAN Y CHROMOSOME

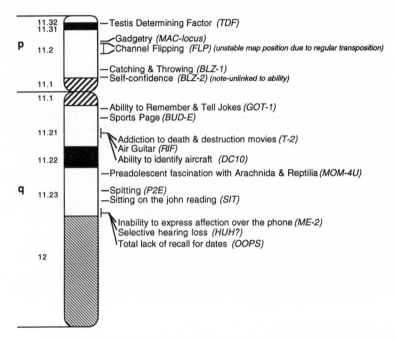

p

11.32
11.31 — Testis Determining Factor *(TDF)*

11.2 — Gadgetry *(MAC-locus)*
Channel Flipping *(FLP) (unstable map position due to regular transposition)*

— Catching & Throwing *(BLZ-1)*
— Self-confidence *(BLZ-2) (note-unlinked to ability)*

11.1

11.1

— Ability to Remember & Tell Jokes *(GOT-1)*
— Sports Page *(BUD-E)*

11.21
Addiction to death & destruction movies *(T-2)*
Air Guitar *(RIF)*
Ability to identify aircraft *(DC10)*

11.22
— Preadolescent fascination with Arachnida & Reptilia *(MOM-4U)*

q

11.23 — Spitting *(P2E)*
— Sitting on the john reading *(SIT)*

Inability to express affection over the phone *(ME-2)*
Selective hearing loss *(HUH?)*
Total lack of recall for dates *(OOPS)*

12

me to only one explanation. I can find nothing else that explains Male Answering Syndrome (the inclination to answer all questions within earshot; a correct answer is not required) or why women shop but men *get*. The only theory that explains all the known facts is that the evolutionary process has led not to a difference among the *Homo sapiens,* but to an entirely *different* species: *Homo slobbius.*

"It all makes sense now," you're thinking.

In *Why Can't a Man Be More Like a Woman?,* I present my findings as objectively as possible. I use behavior of the modern male to show how man has a totally different genetic makeup, one that has evolved through time to the point where he is not even the same species as woman.

The book explains *Homo slobbius* behavior through interviews with "expert" men—that is, men who are experts about being men, or about the behavior that distinguishes men from women. My approach to finding substantive answers is something of a cross between the traditional method and a marketer's approach. So while I talk to psychologists and sociologists, I also interview people who really know how men behave—those successfully selling things to them.

For example, to explain why men who don't cook in the kitchen love to cook outside, I've spoken to the president of the company that makes Weber grills. Who would understand the male psyche better than a guy who sells those ubiquitous bowl barbecues to men everywhere? Similarly, to learn why men don't ask for directions when lost, I've interviewed an official at the American Automobile Association—those folks who give us TripTiks detailing how to get from Point A to Point B—and a gas station attendant (men *hate* to ask service station employees for directions; this book explains why).

I begin at the beginning, when man invented fire and started to barbecue. The book then progresses through the dawn of the wheel, the influence of clothing, and the development of tribal rituals. It continues with mating rituals, home life, reproducing the species and communication skills. In the final chapters, I address intelligence and the hope for greater evolution.

Writing this book and the subscription newsletter it's based on, *The Do(o)little Report,* has taught me a great deal about men and relationships. I've learned that understanding, knowledge, and a really good sense of humor can help women appreciate the men in their lives. With that appreciation comes less frustration with the daily challenges of relationships.

So why can't a man be more like a woman? Do we really want him to be? We still need him to kill the spiders in the bedroom and unscrew jar lids that are on too tight. *Vive la différence!*

1

The Dawn of
❧ the Wheel ❧

Wilma Flintstone didn't know how good she had it when Fred's car was foot-powered. Once the wheel was put in motion, the world saw many significant developments—including the invention of the male cave commonly referred to as the "garage"—while the sense of direction gene deteriorated. This chapter explores the influence of the auto on interspecies relationships.

"Honey, wasn't that our turn?"
Why men don't ask for directions

Overheard in space, July 1969:

Neil Armstrong:	"Buzz, where's that AAA TripTik to the Moon? I thought I clipped it to the visor."
Buzz Aldrin:	"We don't need directions. Turn left at the next meteor."
Armstrong:	"That doesn't feel right to me. Weren't we supposed to veer right as soon as it got dark? Where *is* that thing?"

Aldrin: "Don't worry. We might get to the flag-
                       raising ceremony a little late, but we'll
                       get there. Hey—check the radio for a
                       game, would you?"

The astronauts did eventually make history as the first Earth-
lings to walk on the moon, but only because Armstrong waited
until Aldrin fell asleep, then called a female staffer at Mission Control for directions.

Moonwalker Armstrong is part of a minority. He's a man who
asks for directions when lost. Why are so many others so reluctant
to admit they don't know how to get where they want to go?

Male ego.

According to psychologist John Gray, bestselling author of *Men
Are from Mars, Women Are from Venus,* men pride themselves
on being able to get from Point A to Point B. If they can do that,
they're competent. If they can't they're incompetent. To be lost is
to admit you're incompetent. "For millions of years, women have
selected men based on competency and skills," Gray explains. "A
man knows that if a woman doesn't see him as competent, she
won't select him."

Gray tells a story about how he once got lost when dating the
woman who was to become his wife. "I wanted to impress her by
taking her to a resort, but I made a wrong turn and we ended up *in
the wrong state!* I was embarrassed and humiliated. But she ral-
lied and said, 'I don't know where we are either, but this is so beau-
tiful that I'd like to come back here another time!' I was so
impressed with her graciousness that I thought, 'Now here's a
woman I could spend the rest of my life with,' " Gray admits.

The psychologist tells another story about how he got lost
after he married this thoughtful woman. She was so frustrated
she insisted Gray stop and ask for directions. At a service station, Mrs. Gray said to the attendant, "We're lost! We need to
find this place." The attendant said smoothly, "I know how to get
there." Gray's wife, ecstatic, shrieked, "You do? Oh you're so
wonderful! We're so lucky to have found you!" Sitting in the car

with a bruised ego, Gray mumbled, "Great. Why doesn't he join us and you can dance with *him?*"

As if we gals don't put enough pressure on these poor souls, they also have their own genetic programming to deal with. Gray believes the importance of knowing how to get from here to there is encoded in male DNA because it was crucial to survival. "For thousands of years, directions were very important to hunters. Men were going out for miles and miles, for hours and hours, looking for food. If one didn't have a good sense of direction, he couldn't get home with the food," Gray explains. Then, an enterprising cavewoman invented the compass and cavemen everywhere had to create new excuses for staying out all night.

Does all this mean that a guy without a good sense of direction isn't a "real man"? Men think so, but women don't. But what counts here is what the man thinks. He really believes we'll think he's a loser if he admits he's lost.

Fortunately, there's help. Tom Schroder, an important executive with the American Automobile Association's Florida branch, is in the business of helping men find themselves. "What women can't understand is the challenge of fighting your way to where you want to be," he explains. "To consult with others, to look at maps, would be beneath our warrior selves." Still, AAA provides detailed maps with highlighted routes for those secure enough to ask for assistance.

Bill Adams, manager of the Mobil Mart in Fairport, New York, says men don't like to ask him for directions. "It's the macho image—as in 'I know where I'm going,'" he confides. Adams was unaware of a study revealing that men don't like to ask male service station attendants for directions because the attendants often don't know how to get there either, but are too embarrassed to admit it. Rather than say, "Golly, gee, I don't know," they give bad directions, and the poor lost soul is worse off than he was before.

What's a woman to do? Suck up, says psychologist Gray. "Be supportive. Ask yourself, 'What's more important—getting there, or my partner's feelings?'"

Here are a few more tips to get you where you're going on time:

- Once lost, say you have to use a bathroom and get directions inside.
- Call ahead for directions and memorize them. When he makes a wrong turn, experience a sudden *déjà vu* and get him back on track.
- Use a respectful tone when saying things like, "Honey, wasn't that our turn?"
- Never grab a map from the glove compartment and start yelling.
- Ask him to get directions "as a favor to you" before leaving.
- Insist you need to practice parallel parking and drive yourself.

For their part, men need to realize that we're attracted to a cute butt, an ability to change motor oil, and the inner strength needed to rid a home of rodents. If we were attracted to men because of their sense of direction, we'd all still be wandering the desert with Moses.

"My Problem and How I Solved It"

My husband cannot be trained to rinse his bright blue mouthwash down the sink after he spits it out, so I face a collection of blue-stained globs every morning. Rather than stare at them, I scrub them loose with my husband's toothbrush, then rinse them down the drain myself.

Nancy K., Rochester, Minnesota

True Story

First there were maps. Then came map software for autos. Now there's a voice-activated navigation system for your car. Tell it where you are—if you can figure that out—and where you want to go, and it will give you detailed directions. No doubt this gadget will be marketed to men—only a guy would pay $500 for the hardware and $29 per metropolitan area for CDs rather than pull into a gas station and ask for directions.

STUPID MEN TRICK

You're a savvy, international traveler. You check out of your luxurious London hotel at 12:30 A.M. thinking it's 6 A.M., because you're wearing your watch upside down.

The garage as a sacred place

You've seen at least one in your life—a garage organized beyond belief. There's a nook and cranny, hook and shelf for everything that represents manhood. It is a temple to the God of Mufflers, a god who doesn't like women in his space.

What *is* it with the garage?

Tom Powell, a sociologist teaching at the University of Southern Colorado, believes the garages of the twentieth century replace the barns of the agrarian society before the Industrial Revolution. When Americans were farmers, Powell says, they kept the animals in separate shelters. As a bonus, the man could also retire there for a little peace and quiet. As families migrated to cities for factory jobs, men gave up their barns—and their hiding places. Creating a substitute was inevitable.

Time to build the garage.

"The primary function of the garage was to protect the car," Powell explains, "but its secondary role was as a hiding place for the guy in trouble." Judging by the amount of clutter in many, garages also became storage places for the industrial society's newfound material wealth.

Les Schmeltz of Bettendorf, Iowa, author of *Secrets of Successful Garage Sales,* has examined that wealth in more than 5,000 garages. His extensive personal contact with garages compels him to suspect that men dominate that area only after giving up on the house. "It's a control thing," he explains.

When Schmeltz was young, his mother didn't know how to drive, so she never had a reason to enter the garage. Which was just as well, Schmeltz explains, because it was a place where his father "could retreat and have his kingdom." One can only imagine why the senior Schmeltz would choose a dark, dirty, smelly cavern with a cement floor for his kingdom, while others choose the bathroom to install their thrones.

The garage has been Bill Hoctor's sacred place since he acquired one twenty-four years ago. Recently retired, Hoctor characterizes his garage as "unorganized clutter" and likes it that way. The garage gives him a place to spread out while working on motorcycles, bicycles, cars, and "anything else that needs fixing." That's precisely why it needs to remain his personal and private space.

"It's very disturbing when you're working on something and you lay your tools down and the next day they're gone," he explains from his home south of Buffalo, New York. His wife isn't messing with them, though. She stays out of the garage except to get her garden tools. They're stored well away from her husband's work area, which takes up any space the couple might have used for a car. It's Hoctor's twenty-five-year-old son, who also works on motorcycles, who messes with senior Hoctor's mess.

"I once wanted him to be an acolyte in the sacred garage, but his stuff is in the way of my valuable motorcycles and cars, and I want him out!" Hoctor asserts.

Sociologist Powell suggests other reasons why men select the garage as their personal space:

- They're always in there anyway getting tools for "honey-do" projects.
- They can avoid conversations with women.
- It provides the atmosphere needed to invent things such as microwave popcorn or the remote control.
- It's a place to make rude noises without being detected.

Powell also remembers the fellow who kept his wife out of the garage because that's where he hid his *Penthouse* collection and a companion six-pack of beer. So, fellows, don't drive by that next garage sale. You never know what you might find stashed behind those priceless black velvet paintings in the corner.

"My Problem and How I Solved It"

As in most households, the workload in my home is divided unevenly. Early in our marriage, I asked my husband to free me up a little by taking on the responsibility of paying the bills. It seemed like an appropriate task for a man—I wasn't asking him to do anything feminine, so I thought it was a reasonable request.

He assured me that he could not be trusted with such a major responsibility. Why, he couldn't even remember to log the checks he wrote in his checkbook!

Initially, I accepted that response, but as I grew more pressed for time, and got a little smarter, I decided there was no good reason for him to *not* pay the bills. I used a little trick I've seen work quite well with men—I feigned incompetence in the bill-paying department. Suddenly, I was not making deposits quickly enough. I was missing payments, so we were getting hit with late charges. Why sometimes, I couldn't even find the book with the mortgage coupons! Holy cow! What was happening to me? I didn't know, but I was certainly most apologetic. Guess I was just losing it.

After six weeks of this Academy Award–winning performance, my husband took over the bill-paying.

Deborah B., Odenton, Maryland

True Story

I was impressed with the way my retired husband fixed his lower denture when a tooth fell out. He took it directly to the dental laboratory, but was told he'd have to see a dentist first. My husband, a great guy for eliminating the middleman, went to the drugstore instead and bought a kit used to repair loose dentures. He modeled a tooth out of the material enclosed, and fit it into the hole where his tooth had fallen out. He glued it in, and is now very proudly showing off his new *pink* tooth!

Stupid Men Trick

It's spring cleaning time. To clean out the garage, cover your car hood, roof, and trunk with blankets. Then load items from the garage floor onto the blankets. Back this "mobile shelf" out of the garage slowly, and you're all set to sweep and hose the floor. Works great, too, when you need space for a garage sale.

"I'll wait for you in the car!"

Michael McDermott has at least eight bottles of nail polish in his glove compartment, each used just once.

"My wife is chronically late, so she does her nails in the car," he moans. His wife's tardiness frustrates McDermott so much that he can no longer wait for her in the house. He sits quietly in the car, pacified by the radio.

"I'll wait for you in the car!" has become the male mantra of the nineties. And men have chanted themselves into believing that it will *actually make us hurry and be ready on time!*

McDermott, a writer living in Carmel, New York, admits he wasn't always a car waiter. "When we were first married, I waited by the bedroom door, thinking it would make a difference. Then I moved to the front door. Then I waited in the lobby of our apartment building. Now, fifteen years and four kids later, I'm waiting in the car." McDermott backs the car out of the garage, loads the children, leaves the car running, and sits there with his wife's door open. "Invariably, it never helps," he sighs.

Kirk Starczewski, an antsy college administrator in Saratoga Springs, New York, admits that waiting in the car helps him deal with the frustration of not leaving when he wants to. "If I stand around watching her, I get more and more nervous," he explains. "At least I can turn the car radio on and listen to a decent song."

"I relax and listen to the radio," confirms Bob Gately, a retired civil engineer living in Hopedale, Massachusetts, adding with an equally practical observation, "In the winter, waiting in the car also warms it up."

One observer of the human race believes waiting in the car has less to do with how much time women need to get ready, and more with "the specific domains of the genders." Thomas DePiero, a cultural critic with the University of Rochester in Rochester, New York, says men aren't trying to hurry women when they wait in the car. Instead, "they're getting into more comfortable space. Having the car running is a decoy," he explains, "because it distracts from the issue of space."

DiPiero compares the man in the driveway with the man waiting in the car while the woman is in a grocery store—the store is not his domain any more than the bedroom is when she's getting ready to go out. So why isn't he waiting in front of the TV set, sprawled in the most comfortable chair in the house with a beer in one hand and the remote control in the other? Because he's turned everything off so the little woman will have nothing left to do when she finally *is* ready to head out. "I make sure there's no excuse for her to use," confides McDermott. "I lock all the doors, close all the windows, turn off the TV, and find all the kids' shoes so we're ready when she is. I don't know how much time I really save, but I have the moral high ground," he adds.

Starczewski says that doesn't work in his house. "My wife can be totally ready before the rest of us even start, but she's still the last one out the door. She has to do all those motherly things herself," he says. Starczewski, who likes to arrive on time, has learned through trial and error how to minimize his frustration. He tried adjusting his own timetable, getting himself ready later than usual. Didn't help. He has since worked to get as much control of the schedule as possible. If they need to be at a restaurant by 7 P.M., he tells her they have to be there at 6:30 P.M. "This helps me feel less anxious," he says. McDermott does that too, but complains that he's in control of the social calendar "only on rare occasions."

Men just can't relate to the process women go through to "get ready." As Starczewski notes, men "s--t, shower, and shave in fifteen minutes." No makeup to fuss with. No hair to style. No nails to polish. No need to accessorize. No slip too long for the dress it took fifty-five minutes to select.

I can't help but wonder what would happen if a man went through this uniquely female process just once. Chances are, he'd be so happy to wait in the car quietly the next time that he'd buy you that gift you've always wanted for your birthday: a really good car radio.

"MY PROBLEM AND HOW I SOLVED IT"

It's hard for anyone to remember phone messages, but it seems to be particularly difficult for men. I buy phone message pads in an office supply store and put them next to the home telephone. This has increased the number of messages I ultimately receive by 50 percent—which means I receive 50 percent of my messages now. It's an improvement.

Barbara J., Ogden, Utah

TRUE STORY

Spotted by one of our roving readers on a car's bumper: ALL MEN ARE IDIOTS AND I MARRIED THEIR KING!

STUPID MEN TRICK

Here's a tip for people who wear white oxford cloth shirts to work. Don't worry about ink stains. Just cover them with White-Out. (Nobody will know if you don't tell them.)

2

Men Make
❧ Fire ❧

Way back around the dawn of time, men went out to kill the mastodons while women did the cooking. But in recent centuries, more and more women have joined the ranks of the mastodon hunters, leaving the homefires unattended. To survive, increasing numbers of men have had to cook their own meals (I use the term "cook" quite loosely). Let's examine the male's preferred food, ways of preparing it, and ways of eliminating it.

Why men barbecue

Why is it that a man who wouldn't be caught dead simmering with a saucepan at the stove claims the outdoor grill as his domain? There are as many theories as there are aprons with funny sayings.

"Deep down, where it counts, men know they have been pushed out of the kitchen," says Guy Simpson, recognized among competitive barbecuers as "The K.C. Rib Doctor." "They've been brought up to think that cooking is not a manly thing to do," Simpson explains, "but it's a manly man who can barbecue."

Paul Kirk, another competing outdoor chef dubbed "The Baron

of Barbecue," agrees. "It's a masculine, backwoods type of thing. It's outdoors, in man's territory."

According to research by The Kingsford Products Company, 62% of the outdoor cooking is done by men, versus 24% by women. (We can only assume that the remaining 12% of the grills are tended by male dogs, aliens, or male-female teams.)

James Stephen, President of Weber-Stephen Products Company, maker of the ubiquitous Weber grills, relates the male need to barbecue to the male ego. "When you do it well, people congratulate you," he explains.

"To go to the root of it," agrees Simpson, "I get personal satisfaction out of having people say what a wonderful job I've done. It's kind of an ego trip." The satisfaction one gets from preparing a perfectly charred medium-rare steak must differ from the pleasure one might derive from the moans of delight elicited by a superb *boeuf bourguignon* prepared in the kitchen.

Gary Merrill, who co-hosts a TV show on outdoor cooking, believes grilling is yet one more manly way for men to show off. "It's simply another macho outdoor sport. You've always got your neighbor to compete with."

David Brain, assistant professor of sociology at the New College of the University of South Florida in Sarasota, believes the satisfaction comes from the pomp and circumstance associated with cooking out. "Barbecuing has a ritual quality to it, so the ceremonial head of the family takes charge of the ceremony," he explains, comparing it to the way the man of the house carves the Thanksgiving turkey at the head of the table.

Brain describes barbecuing as a "cheap and dramatic way" to make an occasion special, especially when entertaining. He knows this from experience. Brain recalls what happened after he accepted his first academic position at the University of Indiana. "My wife and I were horrified when we discovered that the biggest social occasion was inviting people over for elaborate meals. We hadn't mastered those skills, so the barbecue solution was simple, but respectable," he says.

Perhaps one of the unconscious motivations for barbecuing goes back to the caveman's primal social scene: hanging out around the campfire with his cave buddies. "If men like to stand around the fire, it's because it's interesting to watch. Fire is associated with power and the center of the tribe—it is the symbolic focal point for maleness," Brain explains.

Doesn't the smoke get in their eyes?

"Not stepping too far away from the smoke is macho," the sociologist points out. "It's an old Boy Scout camping thing, and I know that because I've done it with my son. You sit around the fire and pretend the smoke doesn't bother you."

Yet smoke does provoke a tribal ritual somebody will soon set to music for a debut on MTV. Brain describes it: "That's when all the guys get a beer, stand by the grill, and do that little grill dance. The wind blows the smoke in their eyes, and they all shuffle one way. Then it blows back and they all shuffle back the other way. It really does become rhythmic, with the wind blowing this way and that with regular timing."

For real men such as Paul Kirk and Guy Simpson, barbecuing has moved beyond an excuse to grunt around a fire. As competitive barbecuers, this hobby-turned-passion threatens to take over their lives. Or at least their backyards. Simpson has installed a barbecue pit the size of a bass boat in his yard, using it for his own pleasure as well as for a part-time catering business. Some hobby.

"People with bass boats spend $20,000 on the boat and another $30,000 on the big Suburban to haul it. So for $50,000, they go out on a lake all day, drink beer, and try to catch something. If they do, they turn it in, and maybe win a 35-cent ribbon. I spend the day cooking at my pit, but what a wonderful day I've had, and at the end, I have a string of ribs," Simpson explains.

What's more, producing that string of ribs has all the challenge that any man could want. "Part of the lure has to do with the trick of getting the charcoal started, and knowing the right moment to put the meat on and just how long to leave it on," says sociologist Brain while confessing he hasn't perfected the art. "Oh, I have mastered the fire-building skill, and I can make stuff burn, but I can't cook it properly."

Entertaining with food also says things about your taste and cultural competence, so you have to speak that language fluently. In barbecuing circles, that relates to tools, special effects from wood chips, and flavorful marinades. The man with the biggest tools, the most dramatic effects, and the tastiest secret sauce is certain to impress the most.

While men may say they barbecue because they like to play with fire, reap compliments, or bond around the grill, most eventually will admit that barbecuing separates the men from the gals, who are indoors with the other food. Food historian Lorna Sass, quoted in the *Chicago Tribune,* says this goes back to the days of hunters and gatherers, when men were responsible for hunting, butchering, and cooking the meat, while women were in charge of gathering the greens.

Today, however, it's just another excuse for the guys to congregate without women, and actually look good in the process. While the women keep each other company in the kitchen, the men are allowed to segregate themselves outside because they're cooking dinner. We must recognize that it *is* a team process, with each player offering the head chef tips or advice.

We don't mind. Let them gather without us 'round the grill—at least we get a break from the stove, and isn't that what this is all about, anyway? And while the men are bonding around the flames, we'll prop the camcorder on a windowsill and videotape their "little grill dance" to the Mills Brothers singing "Smoke Gets in Your Eyes." Watch for it on MTV this fall.

"MY PROBLEM AND HOW I SOLVED IT"

Manly man that he is, my husband doesn't worry about safety when he barbecues. If a charcoal grill isn't heating up the way he'd like, he'll shoot lighter fluid directly on the hot coals, oblivious to the fact that the fluid can catch fire, causing the container to explode in his face.

Likewise, when lighting a gas grill, he has been known to let the gas accumulate under the hood before hitting the ignition switch. *Sayonara,* eyebrows!

I've told him that I'm afraid I'll have to visit him in the burn unit of the hospital soon, but that doesn't change his fearless fire-making methods. He also doesn't want me to take over the barbecuing. All I can do now is pull the grill far away from the house when it's time to cook, and make sure his life insurance policy is paid up.

Bonita J., Los Angeles, California

TRUE STORY

After arriving at a beach house for a week's vacation, the family went to the supermarket. While the husband loaded the cart, the wife expressed concern that they were buying too much for one week, especially since she didn't want to spend her evenings cooking. Her husband told her not to worry about it as he tossed steaks and chicken breasts into the cart—he would cook on the grill for the family every night.

Once the food was unpacked and everyone settled in, the husband asked, "Anyone want to go out to dinner?"

STUPID MEN TRICK

Need croutons for your salad? Add zest with the crumbs from your toaster oven.

The four major male food groups

I heard two middle-aged women conspiring at a bridal shower recently. Seems they didn't like their nephew's fiancée, so they bought her the thickest cookbook they could find. "Ha, ha, it will just take up a lot of space in her kitchen because she'll never need to use it," they snickered. Little did the naive bride-to-be know that she could feed her husband beer, cereal, pizza, and beer three times a day and he'd be happy as a slug.

Years ago, as blushing brides, women would ask their adoring husbands each morning, "How does chicken *cordon bleu* sound for dinner tonight, dear?" Daily responses ranged from "Huh?" to "Pizza sounds better," "What kind of cereal do we have?" or "Is there a six-pack in the refrigerator?" In spite of this, women continued to thumb through *Better Homes & Gardens Cookbooks,* searching for mouthwatering, soul-tempting dishes to please their men after a long day on the job. Isn't the way to a man's heart through his stomach?

Maybe not. . . . A recent laboratory study reveals that three out of four men left alone for one week in a well-stocked kitchen will feed themselves what nutritionists now refer to as the four major male food groups: beer, cereal, pizza and beer.* Intrigued by these findings, dietitian Martin Yadrick, a Los Angeles–based spokesperson for the American Dietetic Association, consulted special software to find out if men can survive on this limited diet. Yadrick evaluated the nutritional value of two bowls of Frosted Flakes with two percent milk, five beers, and two slices of pepperoni pizza on regular crust. A real man's diet.

"Overall, it doesn't look too bad!" he says with surprise. "The fiber is inadequate, but substituting high-fiber cereal could fix that. Because most cereal is fortified with vitamins and minerals, there is only one nutrient below the recommended daily allowance: zinc." Consequences of severe zinc deficiency, he notes, include delayed wound healing, anemia, and *hair loss*. (That's probably why the Hair Club for Men advertises on Cheerios boxes.)

Yadrick says the menu he analyzed had only 25 percent of calories from fat. Of course, that's misleading because of the amount of beer consumed. "If the guy drank less beer, the percentage of calories from fat would be higher," he explains. Not likely to happen, though. Information Resources Inc. (IRI), which tracks supermarket spending, notes that men spend three times as much money on beer as women.

Food companies pay experts such as IRI a lot of money to tell them what Americans are eating—and when. For example, Harry Balzer, a consultant with the NPD Group, tells his clients that women still prepare 85 percent of all home meals. *No kidding!* Balzer didn't need to spend weeks monitoring the cooking patterns of households coast to coast for this revelation—all he had to do was ask his mother and her sister Freida. *They* know what's

*Ha, ha. I made this up but it could be true.

going on in today's homes. They also know the day will come when women are too tired, too lazy, or heaven forbid, too belligerent to cook for their men.

We asked Balzer's mother, her sister Freida, and a half dozen other housewives to read a few issues of *Advertising Age, Business Week,* and *Supermarket News,* then brainstorm several "male-friendly" products the big food companies could market when the kitchen revolution takes place. Their list of suggestions shows the uncanny common sense so often overlooked in our society's more experienced women. The ladies quickly picked up on the "megabrand" concept, applying the widely recognized name of one product to as many other products as possible. They also acknowledged the ways in which sister companies owned by the same huge conglomerate could team up with vaguely related cousin products for special pricing or promotions.

Knowing that a single man's idea of a hot dinner is instant oatmeal, our consultants' suggestions also play to the male need for convenience. Their ideas include:

- Domino's Pizza Wheaties
- Pizza Hut Corn Pops Pizza
- A four-product line of Swanson's TV dinners: sausage pizza/Frosted Flakes/Budweiser, Frosted Flakes/sausage pizza/Budweiser, Budweiser/sausage pizza/Frosted Flakes, and sausage pizza/Budweiser/Frosted Flakes
- Post Malt Flakes
- Little Caesars Oatmeal Crust "Pizza Pizza"
- An entire advertising campaign for the American Dairy Association and the Council for Cereal built around celebrity men who eat cereal for supper ("It's not just for breakfast anymore!")
- A 7-Eleven promotion ballyhooing a special price on Golden Crisp, a six-pack of Miller, and a Tombstone pizza purchased together
- A bowl of Cheerios with fruit—and a beer—purchased at a McDonald's drive-through window at dinnertime

Mrs. Balzer and Freida will soon join the ranks of paid consultants advising corporate America on male eating trends. Right now, though, they're busy updating the *Betty Crocker Cookbook*, cutting it from fifteen tabbed categories to four—beer, cereal, pizza, and beer.

"MY PROBLEM AND HOW I SOLVED IT"

I don't know why, but my husband always needs to talk to me when I'm in the upstairs bathroom, in the back of the house and he's in the kitchen cooking. Of course, the fan is on full blast and the hot water is running (because he doesn't know how to turn it off).

The usual routine was for him to holler out a question such as "Where's the pepper?" while I, the enabler, would shout back, "What? What?" before coming downstairs to see what he needed. I've since learned to pretend I don't hear him. Now he just finds it himself—but the water's still running.

Sandra U., Pittsford, New York

TRUE STORY

See if you can find the logic in this: A New Jersey woman went shopping with a friend. When she returned, there was an incredible mess on her kitchen stove. When questioned, her husband explained that he was hungry but didn't want to dirty a pan, so he "grilled" his hot dogs over the open flame on a fork.

STUPID MEN TRICK

In the mood for a gourmet dinner of SpaghettiOs but all the pots are dirty? Just remove the can's label and place it directly on the stove burner.

What a gas!

Gas.

While hard to ignore after a high-fiber dinner with a special guy, it's not something women talk about openly. Yet some of the funniest movie moments have made light of this sensitive subject. (Remember the bean scene in *Blazing Saddles?*) And dozens of greeting cards poke fun at male flatulence. People whisper about it—especially in crowded elevators—but few have the courage to confront it.

We are the first to break the story behind breaking wind. We have uncovered the truth: The gas produced by one man in a single year could fuel a small town for thirty days. An anonymous official at a major Northeastern power company will not share information about his company's research on how to harness this powerful energy source but confirms, "The utility industry is always searching for new and low-cost sources of energy for its customers." He adds, "We are currently investigating a possible partnership with Campbell's Pork and Beans."

Other organizations *are* funding research on the subject. One study proves that the average cow releases 400 liters of methane gas each day. And research by a group of Australian scientists—honest—reveals that men emit intestinal gas twice as often as women do. No kidding! You don't have to be a gastroenterologist to know that men fart more than women, and get more pleasure from it, too. It's practically a folk art for some, passed down from generation to generation. What little boy hasn't learned how to make rude body sounds with his hand, arm, and armpit? (And what little girl hasn't learned to ignore it?)

Men who have lived in college dormitories or military barracks like to retell fascinating stories about how they discovered the gas they emit truly is flammable. "Don't light a match in here!" they chuckle to the waitress when she says today's special is lentil soup. Women don't mind the flammability. It's the noise and odor that do us in. While studies show that smelly chemicals make up just one percent of intestinal gas, any woman trapped in a compact car with a man who has recently dined on corned beef and cabbage will dispute that finding.

Believe it or not, intestinal gas is actually a good sign—it means the gastrointestinal tract is working properly. Too properly, you wonder? The average person passes gas fourteen times a day. Want to "cut" the number down a tad? Read on.

Intestinal gas is caused by undigested food and, to a lesser extent, swallowed air (most of which is belched out, creating more delightful music). Food that isn't digested settles in the colon, where bacteria go to work. The fermentation caused by the bacteria produces (pardon me) gas. Ironically, it's the healthy, high-fiber foods that are good for us that produce much of our gas. In addition, people who are lactose intolerant—they lack enough of the enzyme lactase to break down milk sugar—often suffer painful bouts of gas. Food allergies and antacids also cause problems.

A promising product offers hope for bran bread, broccoli, and brussels sprouts lovers. Called Beano, it's supposed to prevent gas before it starts. Beano is made from a natural food enzyme that breaks down the complex sugars in gassy foods into more simple sugars our bodies can digest. Beano works only if taken with the first mouthful of food.

Problem is, most men aren't bothered by the smells and sounds of flatulence, so they pass by the Beano in the store. That's why women buy 70 percent of the stuff—and cling to it with hope. "Many women have told us this product will save their marriage," says Patti Smith, Beano marketing manager. "Women say they put it on the food before serving it, so their husbands don't even know they're eating it," she adds.

Smith's product might help, but it also would be wise to test your male companion's sensitivity to several types of foods, including vegetables, beans, dairy products, antacids, and carbonated beverages. For example, sometimes just cutting back on the amount of dairy products consumed makes a big difference.

Some physicians recommend eating activated charcoal pills or capsules because charcoal absorbs gas. Simethicone also helps break down large gas bubbles. Soaking and cooking beans, chickpeas, and lentils reduces the substance in these legumes that is responsible for gas. Hiding the laxatives, which can cause gas-trapping bowel spasms, will also help.

Modifying the diet and adding Beano to your food now and then will probably help clear the air in your relationship. But to be safe, we've asked the Beano folks to put noseplugs in the packages.

A ROSE BY ANY OTHER NAME . . .

How many of these phrases for "passing gas" does your companion use?

Barking spiders	Ripping one
Tooting	Stepping on a duck
Cutting the cheese	Talking with the wrong mouth
SBDs (Silent But Deadly)	Wind breakers
Jean heaters	Butt burps
Cheek slappers	Blowing dust
Sparking	One cheek sneak

GOOD NEWS AND BAD NEWS

The good news is these foods are healthful. The bad news is they're gas producers. Mix and match carefully . . . and don't light a match!

Beets	Lettuce
Black-eyed peas	Lima beans
Broccoli	Onions
Brussels sprouts	Parsley
Cabbage	Parsnips
Carrots	Peanuts
Cauliflower	Peas
Chickpeas	Pinto beans
Chicory	Pumpkin
Corn	Red kidney beans
Cucumbers	Spinach
Green beans	Split peas
Green peppers	Soybeans
Leeks	Squash
Lentils	

"MY PROBLEM AND HOW I SOLVED IT"

My husband hasn't mastered the art of leaving the recycled trash on the curb for pickup. He never remembers what day of the week the truck comes—even though it's always the same day. I help him by leaving the blue recycling bin in the middle of his parking space. That way, he can't park his car until he moves the bin. Fortunately, he does take it to the curb. My next goal is to teach him to remember the day all by himself with no help from me.

Doris W., Columbia, Missouri

TRUE STORY

After a particularly "aromatic" session in the bathroom, one man poured Listerine down the toilet. (It's cheaper than after-shave.)

STUPID MEN TRICK

Drat! You're out of milk, cream, even Cremora for your coffee. Don't despair. Add a little mayonnaise (and watch it clump and curdle).

3

From Bearskin
to Polyester

Men and clothes—what a topic! Women need to learn why "You're not wearing *that*, are you?" will never encourage a man to shop the sales for a new work shirt, toss the jersey he's worn since his football team won the county championship, or stop wearing his baseball cap backward. Men place less emphasis on shopping than women do—and it shows. Unless it's a stereo shop or a new car showroom, men are not comfortable in retail locations.

Women shop, men get

Men are doing more grocery shopping either because they're staying single longer, or because their wives work and don't have time to shop. And while a man will spend an entire weekend lurking in stereo shops looking for the perfect sound system for his apartment, he won't spend more than twenty minutes buying a new suit for a job interview. Even then, he wants his girlfriend's opinion. And men as gift shoppers? Forget it. (They do!)

Volumes of market research have been commissioned in recent years to identify the "new male" as an individual who shops. Results confirm what women who spend time in stores know first-hand:

- More men than ever are navigating supermarket aisles in the true hunter-gatherer tradition, but they usually don't have a full cart of groceries and three hyperactive kids hanging off the sides.
- Men are buying more of their own clothes (and they look like it).
- Men have not mastered the art of gift shopping.

Maritz Marketing Research concluded in a 1991 study that one-third of the country's men do all or most of the food shopping for their households. Not so coincidentally, one-third of all men are single. Could it be possible, then—I'm not a market researcher so I hate to jump to conclusions—but could it be possible that these men are food shopping because *there's nobody else to do it?* Of course. This is not a task anyone does voluntarily.

Of the married men, a measly 12 percent do all the food shopping. This is not because women are supermarket martyrs. Women dominate the aisles because they're protecting the family budget from men, who are more likely to food shop in pricier convenience stores, least likely to use cents-off coupons, and spend most of their money on automotive supplies, beer, wine, and shaving needs.

Note that "clothing" is not in that last sentence. It is common knowledge that men do not like to shop for clothes. Martin Pazzani monitors shopping patterns as head of sales and marketing for a television marketing agency that works with home shopping and retail clients. He says that for fashionable women, "shopping is a long, drawn-out process." But men dislike shopping for clothes because clothes are not interesting to them.

Retail humorist Rick Segel learned this the hard way. Segel, who has been in the women's apparel business for nearly a quarter of a century, bought a men's store in its ninety-ninth year. He closed it in its hundredth. Segel tried to sell men's clothes the way he sold women's, but it didn't work.

"Men buy black, brown, and navy replacement clothing," he explains. "For the most part, they want to fit into the crowd and not stand out. The wildest they get is with their tie purchases—it's like they're going off the deep end when they purchase one tie that's nontraditional."

Segel learned that men shop less often than women, but they purchase more items in one visit, usually buying their whole wardrobe for the season in one trip. If they can be outfitted from head to toe in one store, they're as happy as they can get about the shopping experience. Segel didn't realize this when he closed the shoe department in his men's store because it carried just five styles. To Segel, it was a waste of space. "Dumb," he says, laughing. "Men stopped shopping at my store because they couldn't buy their shoes there, too. There's a real psychology to men's retailing," Segel laments with hindsight.

Terry Montlick is a Connecticut computer consultant who epitomizes the male clothing shopper. "I get in and out as quickly as possible before anything bad happens to me," he confides. "I don't browse because shopping is not an entertaining activity. Basically, all I want are the same clothes I bought last year—I'm not even a big believer in seasonal clothing. I wear short sleeves all year, and I don't even care about the color of my shirt as long as it has a functional pocket." For the most part, Montlick, forty-four, wears the same styles he wore in high school.

Not surprisingly, the 1994 Stillerman Jones & Co. National Benchmarks of Shopping Patterns study reveals that men account for just 35 percent of all mall shoppers. Men who *are* at malls are making big-ticket purchases, according to the Maritz study. Almost half of the men surveyed claimed to make the decisions about big-ticket items, including furniture and cars.

Marketer Pazzani observes, "Men shop for cars, but women treat buying a car like an impulse purchase. Unlike many women, some men spend three months going to dealers kicking tires and doing test drives. The difference between a considered purchase and an impulse item is the subject," he asserts.

Pazzani notes that fewer people in general enjoy going shopping now, which is why catalog and TV shopping have become increasingly popular. This is because we have less time for this sport, but also because, Pazzani believes, "Service and knowledge of products at stores is at an all-time low."

But even this male marketing whiz whinces at the subject of men as gift purchasers. "I have to be in the mood for Christmas shopping," he explains cautiously, "and sometimes that's the middle of December and sometimes it's at the very last minute." Pazzani turns this perceived shortcoming into a positive for a mail-order company, however. "One gift company is exploring a service for the last-minute male shopper. The man provides key dates, names, and addresses at the start of the year, and the company sends gifts automatically at the right time." (Perhaps for an extra fee, the delivery person will apply CPR to the woman who has a coronary when she receives a tasteful gift on the day of her anniversary.)

This tendency to shop for gifts too late—or not at all—is not lost on the floral industry, which claims that 25 percent of all flower purchases are to get a man out of trouble. Florists call it—this is not a joke—the "doghouse" business. Since women continue to report that men buy lousy gifts, this is money in the bank for florists. In *The Do(o)little Report*'s first national survey on this subject, one woman complained that her husband gave her a cemetery plot for her birthday; another received a case of motor oil for Christmas. These do not compare with the man who bought his wife an instant camera for her birthday so he could take pornographic pictures of himself for publication. He is now an ex-husband.

Clearly, it's in our own best interest to help men become more interested in shopping. Studies prove that men don't know their way around their own supermarkets, so stores need to offer introductory tours and host seminars on how to compile shopping lists, clip coupons, and tune out whining children (especially one's own). Clothes shopping will never be high on any man's list of fun things to do on a day off, so ask him to browse through catalogs while watching TV (see "Men who can do more than one thing at a time" in Chapter 9). Encourage department stores to hire former professional athletes as clerks in the men's department. Lobby fashion designers to make ratty old T-shirts *de rigueur*. As for getting the gift you want, here are three words of advice: *Buy it yourself.*

TIPS FOR GETTING THE GIFT YOU WANT

- Give your man a wallet-size paper with your clothing sizes and favorite colors.
- Don't expect him to be a mind reader. Compile an annual wish list for all special occasions and post it on the refrigerator.
- Don't trust him to remember all special dates—remind him at least one week in advance.
- To minimize disappointment, remember that gifts are more important to women than they are to men.
- Don't read too much into a bad gift. It usually means that he's careless, not that he doesn't care.
- Forget subtlety. Mark pages in your favorite catalogs and tell your mate any of those items would be great for your birthday.
- Reward him when he actually manages to buy something you'd like. Positive reinforcement works as well with men as it does with children.
- Remind him to keep receipts. You'll need them to make exchanges!

WINNERS FROM THE "WORST GIFT FROM A MAN" CONTEST

The Do(o)little Report received hundreds of entries in its first "Worst Gift from a Man" contest. We solicited entries in three categories: "Dumbest Gift," "Most Inappropriate Gift," and "Gift He Bought for You so He Could Use It." A vast majority of contest entries fell into the last category. Not surprisingly, many of the gifts mentioned were from ex-boyfriends and ex-husbands. Winning entries:

Dumbest Gift

- Two sticks of pepperoni for Mother's Day (when the recipient expressed surprise, her husband responded with pride, "Most women get flowers!")

Most Inappropriate Gift—a Tie

- A sapphire and diamond ring he stole from his mother (this was discovered when the girlfriend visited the mother)
- White Shoulders perfume the boyfriend purchased because he liked the way it smelled on a previous girlfriend

Gift He Bought for You So He Could Use It—a Tie

- A remote-controlled Army tank from a history buff
- Router bits in a velvet-lined box and velvet pouch—he said he would use them to install the paneling she wanted in the house

Honorable Mention

- Several women received life insurance policies naming their husbands as beneficiaries

MEN AS SHOPPERS

American Demographics and *Progressive Grocer* magazines study the male consumer. They tell us that men:

- Who are food shopping are less likely than women to refer to shelf offers or brochures, but more likely to read shopping cart ads and aisle markers.

- Are buying more ties—tie purchases by women have dropped 20 percent in recent years to a total of 60 percent.
- Who are single spend 61 percent of their food budgets away from home, compared to 40 percent for single women.
- Spend the most on automotive supplies, beer, wine, and shaving cream, and the least on cosmetics, sewing notions, and hosiery.
- Say they don't enjoy shopping as much as women say they enjoy it.
- Are less likely than women to use cents-off coupons.
- Spend more money than women do.
- Are manipulated more successfully by children.
- Get more flustered when their children make a scene in a store.
- Spend more time at the supermarket, handle and read more packages, and buy more from floor displays.
- Are more likely than women to food shop in convenience stores.
- As teenagers are half as likely as teenage girls to grocery shop.

"My Problem and How I Solved It"

Did you ever wonder if men think that women have built-in scanners they use to do a quick inventory of the refrigerator and cupboards before going grocery shopping? Why else would men neglect to tell us they used the last stick of butter—the last roll of paper towels—the last drop of mouthwash?

When my husband would say, "Hey, we're all out of skim milk!," I would grumble about how I wish I had known about it when I bought groceries yesterday—then head out to the 7-Eleven to replace the empty container. With age, I have become wiser. Today, if the missing item isn't added to my grocery list by you-know-who, he's the one who goes out in the downpour to replace it. Likewise, I replace whatever I use up.

I don't expect him to do the shopping, but I do expect him to tell me when he needs something. I'm not working for the Psychic Hotline—yet!

Jennifer T., Salt Lake City, Utah

TRUE STORY

It is August 31. The expiration date on the sour cream in his hand is August 7. He says, "Nope, guess I can't use it," and puts it back in the refrigerator.

STUPID MEN TRICK

Iron your shirts by placing them neatly between the mattress and box springs.

WOMEN WANT TO KNOW: INSIGHTS INTO THE MALE MIND, BY ONE WHO'S BEEN THERE

What Is It with Men and Stereos?
by Lee Tougas

Why do men buy stereo equipment? The easy answer is because women won't. If I didn't buy the stereo equipment for our household, my wife and I could never enjoy the true fidelity of Mozart by the Academy of St. Martin in the Fields, the verve of "Take Five" by Brubeck, or the power of the introduction to "Your World Champion, Chicago Bulls"—as if we were there.

True fidelity is the key. Anyone can buy a cassette player and a set of speakers and hear a reasonable facsimile of the real thing. Take the sound of Gloria Estefan in full voice in front of two hundred thousand screaming fans. Without true fidelity, she might sound like Tiny Tim. Without true fidelity, the Big Bang becomes the Little Pop. And Pachelbel's "canons" should only be heard in excess of 200 dB (translation: decibels).

After true fidelity has been established as the objective, which partner is best qualified to achieve that goal? The partner who understands that inductive coupling has nothing to do with sex for bribes, or the one who asks for something in beige and magenta? The one who can distinguish between a tuner/pre-amp/amp combination and receiver, or the one who is intimidated by a 128-function remote? I ask you.

I began assembling our system more than ten years ago. I am now on my third CD unit. (It takes a while to find the right one.) I also own a pair of cables with arrows on them. I never understood the difference in fidelity that occurs when electrons flow in the right direction until I owned a pair of cables with arrows on them. It is not quite the same as playing Beatles records backward, but close. And I am the first one on the block with DAT (translation: Digital Audio Technology). No one else has DAT. I do. The true answer to "Why do men buy stereo equipment?" is the same as the answer to why we don't ask for directions. We don't want to appear stupid to the one we love.

Any man who has walked into a stereo store and seen what money can buy is not going to leave unless he buys something. My wife and I went to a stereo store recently. Met the owner. The store is named after him. I need a headset for the upstairs stereo (that's right, the *upstairs* stereo). He asks, "What do you have?"

"Well," I answer, "I have IMAGE towers on pedestal mounts, Denon POA-4400 single-channel power amplifiers, a Kyocera R-861 receiver, a Denon DCD-1520 CD unit, a Nakamichi RX-202 cassette playback, an AIWA F-990 recording deck, and a Stax SRM-1/Mk-2 dynamic headset."

He's impressed. He asks, "What's your budget?"

"Three hundred dollars," I respond. He laughs ($300 won't come close to covering what I need). Wife faints. We leave with a catalog. Costs $5. I'll be back.*

Men's clothing should be labeled with expiration dates

I realize that, *technically,* the way my husband dresses does not reflect on me. People realize he's a grown-up who can select his own clothing. I know this. Still, I was mortified—absolutely *morti-*

*Lee Tougas is a mechanical engineer—but witty nonetheless.

fied—when he wore his moth-eaten old Little League uniform to his best friend's wedding rehearsal.

Granted, it was a casual gathering. And yes, his friend had even played in Little League with him. The proud father of the groom was also their Little League coach. But, geez. Wasn't I supposed to stop him from walking out the door looking like a fifth grader on testosterone? Isn't that what wives are for?

I am a failure. But I am not alone.

Men everywhere—all over the planet—wear clothes that should have been thrown away years ago. Despite our best efforts, women have not successfully weeded out faded college sweatshirts, shirts with grease stains, khakis thin at the knees, or high school gym shorts. While I admit we've failed, I propose shifting responsibility back where it belongs—to men, and more specifically, the men who make men's clothing. I challenge the men's apparel industry to label clothing with expiration dates. If men can't figure out when to throw out their Farrah slacks, the manufacturers can do it for them.

I tested the concept with Levi Strauss & Co. In an official unprepared statement, spokesman Dave Samson announced, "No, Levi Strauss has never considered putting an expiration date on its men's clothing, and probably won't."

What can you expect from an industry run by men?

These are people who set themselves up to sell to one man maybe just once every five years. They do this by making the same styles in the same fabrics in the same colors year after year after year. *The clothing is never out of style.* As one men's retailer explains it, "You put the clothes out on the floor. When they don't sell, you mark the price down. What's left is stored in the back room. Then you drag it all out again next year, and mark the price back up."

Melvin Weiner, associate professor of apparel at the Philadelphia College of Textiles & Science, explains that, for men's suits at least, there's a good reason why there is such fashion unconsciousness. "There are 120 steps involved in manufacturing a man's jacket. There are half as many involved in a woman's jacket. Every time you make a dramatic fashion change in the design of a man's suit—which is something as simple as making lapels a fraction of an inch wider—it throws the manufacturing process into turmoil."

Connecticut archaeologist Roger "It will be back in style soon" Moeller observes, "If you look at photos of men, you cannot tell by their clothing when the pictures were taken." The same plaid, button-down-collar shirt he wore to the party after his high school graduation is still acceptable fifteen years later, at the reunion cookout.

Richard Martin, curator of the Costume Institute at the Metropolitan Museum of Art in New York City, believes this is one reason why his exhibit is so desperate for men's garments. "Even when it barely fits any longer, there's still a sense of pride in saying they can still wear that letter sweater," he admits. "Men are still trying to be eighteen to twenty-one because those were the best years of their lives."

Moeller, who makes his fashion statements in a battered Sonny Bono sheepskin vest and "comfy" polyester slacks because "they've stretched out in just the right places with bulges in just the right spots," believes hanging on to clothing forever actually gives men a fashion advantage. "If you've been wearing them for a long time and have had guidance from women along the way, you probably know after a few years which items match," he explains.

Weiner argues that men don't throw away old clothes because they can't afford new ones. "Men don't have the disposable income for clothing the way women do," he insists. "Household money for clothing is spent on the children first, then the women. Men come last, if there's anything left over." According to the Consumer Expenditure Survey, American households spend $607 a year on women's clothing, compared with $345 for men's.

But what if—just *what if*—men's clothes had expiration dates? Would men pay attention to them? Archaeologist Moeller warns, "An expiration date usually says 'best if used by.' It doesn't mean you can't keep using it."

If he's right, women will have to continue to be responsible for keeping male wardrobes presentable. For some, this will require professional help. Lisa Kanarek, a Dallas-based organizing consultant and author of *Organizing Your Home Office for Success*, faces this problem frequently with clients battling overflowing closets. Kanarek fantasizes about a collection of matching clothes for men similar to the animal line for children sold years ago by Sears. Instead of matching the tiger on the shirt with the tiger on the pants, the men could match hammers, screwdrivers or saws. The *pièce de résistance* would be the special dyes used on the tools, which fade with repeated washings. "When the hammer is white, the man knows it's time to toss the shirt in the trash," Kanarek proclaims. A more realistic solution, Kanarek admits, is to teach men that when they buy something new, they should throw away something old.

Kanarek and other experts offer these tips for women interested in weeding out clothing that has exceeded expiration dates:

- Display old photos of the man wearing the offending clothes—with huge sideburns and *Saturday Night Fever* jewelry.
- Drip acid on the seams so they disintegrate quicker.
- "Accidentally" splash bleach on the clothes, making them so unattractive even a man wouldn't wear them.
- When he wears a particularly loathsome garment, smile dreamily and say, "My old boyfriend used to have a sweater just like that!"
- Give the old clothing away. He won't argue against helping the homeless.
- Stage a mock robbery, where only the old clothing is stolen.
- When moving to a new address, pack the old clothes in one box and lose it.
- Buy him clothes made of rayon, and wash them with cotton garments so they don't last as long. Buy silk shirts—the cuff edges will split quicker than those made with cotton.
- Turn his clothes into cleaning rags. "More people than you would imagine think the best cleaning device is men's underwear," confesses curator Martin.

Or consider donating the clothing to Martin's Costume Institute. If he can't put it on display, Martin can turn your donation into rags for the maintenance staff. At least *you'll* never have to see them again.

"My Problem and How I Solved It"

Have you ever noticed how when you're really busy, even the littlest inconveniences get to you?

I was tired of taking the time to turn my husband's undershirts right side out for the laundry. I asked him if he would do it himself to save me a few minutes when I washed clothes. He said having his undershirts inside out didn't bother him. Well, if it didn't bother him, it didn't bother me, so I washed, folded, and put away his undershirts the way he put them in the laundry—inside out.

After a few weeks, he finally said, "Why are my undershirts inside out? When I reminded him of our conversation, his response was, "Oh." He's still not turning them right side out before they're washed . . . and neither am I!

Mary Lou F., Cleveland, Ohio

True Story

A busy woman needed to use something to catch urine for a home pregnancy test, so she grabbed a measuring cup. Before running out the door to work, she tossed the cup in the sink, figuring she would wash it that night. When she got home from work she noticed her husband had already made dinner (bless his heart), but that the measuring cup was sitting on the counter with rice stuck to it.

She asked if he had washed the cup first, and—you guessed it— his answer was "Nope!"

She passed on the rice that night!

Stupid Men Trick

Don't throw out a colored garment just because bleach left white spots. Dab at the spot with a matching Magic Marker and— *voilà!*—the spot is gone.

The crowning glory:
Why men wear baseball caps

Babs Richard believes a man's IQ drops 50 points as soon as he puts on a baseball cap. What would she think of my thirty-something neighbor who wears that cap backward as he cruises around the neighborhood on a bicycle? The backward touch must be worth at least another 25-point drop.

We know why big boys wear their caps backward—they want to look like little boys. But why do men wear baseball caps at all? There are practical reasons, of course. A cap is an excellent sunscreen-sunglass combination for the balding fellow. Health-conscious men claim the shade of the brim protects their faces from the sun's harmful rays. Others are honest enough to admit they wear caps on "bad hair days."

Utah writer Dennis Hinkamp believes the popularity of caps is linked to an increased interest in tattoos. "We have run out of advertising space on our T-shirts and jean pockets, so the head and body are the next logical places," he insists. Steven Stark writes in *The Atlantic* that caps are indicative of a "nostalgic return to early adolescence."

But the most common reason, according to the company that makes more licensed baseball caps than any other in the country, is sports related. According to Joe Trimboli, director of marketing and sales for New Era Cap Co., "Stalwart, die-hard sports fans wear team hats to show their support.

"We all probably had baseball heroes," reminisces Trimboli, "so in one small respect, maybe we think this is good for our image, that it will help us be more like that hero. And some men, I'm sure, probably think wearing an official cap—the kind the pros wear—will help them play better." New Era's caps are part of the official Major League Baseball uniform, the only sport requiring players to wear hats. The company also is licensed to make fan caps for pro baseball, football, and basketball teams.

Luca Rensi, a young publishing executive in New York City, wears caps constantly, but there's no sports connection for him. "I wear them if my hair's messed up or to keep the sun off my face. When I don't want to be recognized, I add a pair of sunglasses and I can be a fly on the wall," he explains.

"You can tell something about the person by his cap," observes Billy Richard, an insurance executive in Charlotte, North Carolina, and husband of the aforementioned Babs. "Myself, I'm a fabric snob. I wear only cotton and wool caps—no polyester or mesh." Richard selects only presized caps as well, eschewing the more common adjustable plastic tab style favored by John Deere drivers.

Is there a caste system among cap wearers, perhaps?

Trimboli at New Era Cap thinks not. He says the 100 percent wool, sized caps are what the real baseball players wear, and that's why they are preferred by so many enthusiasts.

Richard, who owns twenty-five caps but wears just five regularly, is remarkably introspective about the role of the baseball cap in his wardrobe *and* his life. He wears a hat to escape the expectations others have of him as chief financial officer of his company. "When I put that cap on, I get to be a little kid again," he admits, noting that most of the men at his professional level probably don't wear caps as much as he does.

"That's why I can also blend in more when I wear one," explains the man whose fortieth birthday party invitation read "Baseball cap required." "I can wear a cap and a T-shirt to a bar, and I'm just a good ol' boy like the rest of them. This gives me more opportunities and flexibility than the guy in the corner with his Ralph Lauren shirt."

One Pennsylvania executive makes a statement with baseball caps on the job every day. A labor negotiator who is not bald, he wears a cap all the time—in his office, in his boss's office, in negotiations. The caps represent teams from cities where he has lived. It's likely he uses them to communicate to the blue-collar workers he negotiates with: "Don't let this tie fool you—I'm more like you than you think."

Marketer Trimboli has learned that a cap also can attract attention—something every man welcomes. He had a cap made for his alma mater, Williams College, featuring the school mascot, a purple cow. It caught the eye (head?) of baseball star Bucky Dent, who insisted he had to have one. A trend was born.

Men know lots about baseball caps except how to use them to capture the attention of women. Some advice: View them as fashion accessories, not devices for covering thinning hair. On a date, match the color of your cap with the color of your T-shirt (fashion tip: black goes with everything). If you long for a classy chick, go upscale with sized caps in natural fabrics. And by all means, wear *only* what the pros wear. Otherwise, your cap won't have any affect on your softball game. Then we gals will know you're just wearing a cap 'cause you're bald.

"MY PROBLEM AND HOW I SOLVED IT"

My husband seemed to get pleasure from walking past the pile of clean folded clothes on the stairs. I would ask him repeatedly to take them upstairs when he walked by them. Finally, I asked him why he didn't just carry them up automatically.

"There's no sign on them that says 'take me upstairs,' " he responded.

Well, there is now!

Roberta S., Rochester, New York

TRUE STORY

As a regular blood donor, a young woman wondered why her husband never went to the blood bank. "Have you ever given blood?" she asked. "No," he replied, "because my first wife was anemic."

STUPID MEN TRICK

If your favorite shirt is in the dirty clothes basket, just toss it in the dryer with a fabric softener sheet for ten minutes. (Note to fellows: This will not make a dirty shirt look better. The shirt will only smell better.)

❉ 4 ❉

Tribal
❧ Rituals ❧

☙❧

Male tribal rituals exist to exclude females. Since the dawn of time, men have observed women's lack of affinity for gadgets and team sports. Hence, men embrace technology and athletics with strong hairy arms to keep women at a distance.

Distant replay: Why men set the VCR to tape games they attend

Sports widows understand the problem. "Charlie" has been gone all day at a football game. When he finally gets home, you're ready for a hug and adult conversation.

Forget it. He has taped the game and wants to relive every action-packed moment as soon as he gets in the door.

Call it the game from hell. The game that wouldn't go away. It's *the game on videotape,* and your male companion plays it over, and over, and over, as if the sporting event actually has a major role in the grand scheme of life.

You can't help but wonder, *Do men really have to tape games they attend?* Of course not. Is it possible to understand why they do it? Maybe. Can we accept it as normal behavior? I doubt it.

43

So why do they do it?

Buffalo Bills fan Dirk Schumacher has made the ninety-minute trek to every Buffalo home game from suburban Rochester, New York, since 1978. He videotapes each game. Once back home, he breezes past the wife and kids to rewind the tape. "I like to hear what the announcers say about the plays," he explains.

My husband, Bill Assimon, drives two hours to every Syracuse University home basketball game at least one night a week—sometimes two—during upstate New York's often brutal winter season. He tapes, too. "Taping lets us view the instant replay of a controversial call or particularly exciting play," he says.

A less serious fan—or a normal person—might wonder why they just don't stay home and watch the game on TV.

Rudy Martzke, who writes the "Sports on TV" column for *USA Today,* believes "it all boils down to the difference between men and women. I'm not saying we should be proud of this, but attending the game is part of the male bonding experience. It's part of our love affair with sports. We want to go to events together, sit together, cheer on our team together. We like to moan when our team does badly. The VCR is an extension of that love affair with sports and the teams we back."

Martzke doesn't want to miss the "fun, joy, and excitement of the crowd" so he attends the game. He "keeps the excitement going" back home by watching the game again on tape.

"It's much more exciting when you attend—you get all caught up in the excitement and emotion of the game," Schumacher says. For Assimon, it's also a social occasion. "There's a stronger sense of camaraderie at the game. You can meet with friends for a meal beforehand, and sit together while you experience an event that is often electric."

Assimon adds that spouses "don't let you express yourself freely at home." He defines free expression as yelling at the players as if they can hear you, suggesting creative movements for the referees, and throwing anything within reach at the coach on the screen.

To put his behavior in perspective, Assimon offers a story of somebody who's worse—a friend who tapes Syracuse football games. "He spends several hours at the game, then goes home to actually chart the plays while he replays the event. This lets him study the coach's strategy," he says, noting that it also gives his friend's wife time to study divorce papers.

Martzke also welcomes the opportunity to savor the moment on a bad TV night, when his wife dismisses him to the second television set. There, remote control in hand, he is happy to play and replay the NCAA Final Four basketball tournament, the Super Bowl, or the Rose Bowl.

"The more seriously you take the sport, the more likely you are to tape the games," Assimon observes. Let's see. You have to be obsessed to do it, and some are more obsessed than others. Proof, once again, that there are varying degrees of insanity.

REAL MEN HAVE THESE GAMES
ON VIDEOTAPE

Baseball
Game 6, 1986 World Series, New York Mets vs. Boston Red Sox

Game 1, 1988 World Series, Los Angeles Dodgers vs. Oakland A's

Game 6, 1993 World Series, Toronto Blue Jays vs. Philadelphia Phillies

Pro Football
1982 Super Bowl XVI, San Francisco 49ers vs. Cincinnati Bengals

1991 Super Bowl XXV, Buffalo Bills vs. New York Giants

College Football
1992 Orange Bowl, University of Miami vs. Nebraska University

1987 Fiesta Bowl, Penn State vs. University of Miami

College Basketball
1983 NCAA championship game, North Carolina State vs. University of Houston

1985 NCAA championship game, Villanova University vs. Georgetown University

1987 NCAA championship game, Syracuse University vs. Indiana University

Pro Basketball
Game 6, 1980 NBA championship game, Los Angeles Lakers vs. Philadelphia 76ers

Throughout the 1980s, NBA championship games, Los Angeles Lakers vs. Boston Celtics

Olympics
1980 USA vs. USSR hockey game—"Miracle on Ice"

Tennis
1980 Wimbledon championship, Bjorn Borg vs. John McEnroe

"MY PROBLEM AND HOW I SOLVED IT"

My husband was watching a football game when I wanted him to go shopping with me. He said there were just fifteen minutes left. Those fifteen football minutes took forty-five real minutes. He said, "That's football time."

When we went shopping, I told him I'd be out in fifteen minutes. I came out two hours later. I said, "That's shopping time."

Claudia S., Long Island, New York

True Story

Although he was asleep on the couch, the man picked up the remote and started surfing—with one eye sort of open. When his wife went to take the remote away from him so she could continue watching a program, he grunted and took it back—and promptly fell back asleep! We need to warn the rest of the world about this phenomenon—*sleep surfing!*

Stupid Men Trick

Geez—you'd better wash all those dishes before your wife comes back from a week-long trip to her mother's! Haul them to the bathtub, pour liquid detergent all over them, and run the shower for thirty minutes.

WOMEN WANT TO KNOW: INSIGHTS INTO THE MALE MIND, BY ONE WHO'S BEEN THERE

Channel Surfing USA
by Steve Crane

Archaeologists discovered an ancient cuneiform tablet from the year 2312 B.C. on which a Sumerian woman had written what has become known in scholarly circles as "The Woman's Lament." It reads, "I talk. He nods. O Life!" Evidently, Sumerian males were just like us: Decent, hardworking guys intent on finding the perfect beer. So who knows why men zap channels? The real mystery is, why don't women?

To sit and watch something I don't want to watch and don't have to watch when, at the end of my fingertip, rests the consumer electronics version of the neutron bomb—capable of wiping out with the merest touch of my digit whole high-rises packed with snot-nosed advertising copywriters—well, you can see the attraction, right?

No, probably not. My wife is perfectly comfortable serving as a target for some moron's mindless advertising dart. She says, "TV's a distraction anyway. What difference does it make what's on?" I say, "Engage me, or die!"

But lest you suspect this is degenerating into a diatribe against womankind's passivity in the face of Madison Avenue's insults, I have a surprise for you. Truth is, this dilemma has been misinterpreted from the first, though understandably enough since the zapper has the makings of a power tool. And since men are the undisputed masters of this tool (it's doubtful any woman has an operator's license from the FZZ—something all men carry with childlike pride, right next to their fishing license and a picture of Mom), the world has concluded that this is one more example of what has gotten us into all the trouble we've *ever* been in: the male animal's unregenerate hunger for power and his restless desire to use it.

Wrong. Zapping points to an essential weakness in the male character, not strength. It is because we find it so difficult to concentrate our own minds that we need an instrument like the channel changer. Or more properly, the television. Television engages our interest so completely because we lack the woman's ability to do it ourselves. Unable or unwilling to keep our minds occupied through self-generated interest, we become fickle and demanding and dissatisfied.

Enter the channel changer. It allows us to remain engaged by constantly serving up "change." It generates interest by generating images. It gives us a sense of control while disguising the truth of our own powerlessness.

In short, it caters to us. Since you won't.*

Bubba, Bonzo, and Biff:
Why men give each other nicknames

Here's a joke popular with men: *Question:* Why do men nickname their penises? *Answer:* They don't want a stranger doing 95 percent of their thinking!

I had my first insight into the significance of male nicknames during my freshmen year of college. A guy in my dorm was particularly proud of the quilt his younger sister had made for him be-

*Steve Crane recently won his neighborhood's channel-surfing competition. He was sponsored by Ocean Pacific sportswear.

cause stitched into the center was his high school nickname: *T-Bone*. It was obvious the nickname was as treasured as the handmade comforter, but I did not know why.

I entered college without a nickname. I left college without a nickname. But during those four years, I learned enough about this male shorthand to dish out countless monikers to my three roommates—*Bronxie, Shimmy-Shimmy,* and *Bux*—and to teach them how to assign nicknames to the crop of *really cute* guys we yearned to date. Our bathroom wall had a "Hunk List" of pet names ranging from *Green Peas* to *Cal from Afton*. This code allowed us to discuss these hunks anywhere without embarrassment. It served us well.

Men use nicknames for other reasons. Ira *The Assassin** Bachrach, president of NameLab, Inc., a San Francisco company that develops names for products and businesses, has learned it's a form of male shorthand. "Men assign familiar words to things that are so common in their lives that they have to say them very often. It's their form of abbreviated speech," he explains.

Bachrach illustrates this male tendency with the one-syllable words guys use to describe their two primary interests: beer and sports. A bottle of Budweiser is a *Bud*. A Michelob is a *Mick*. The Seattle Mariners are the *M's*. The Oakland Athletics are the *A's*. The New York Knickerbockers are the *Knicks*. You will indeed be hard-pressed to find a professional team with a nickname containing more than two syllables. While to some this might illustrate intellectual shortcomings or vocabulary difficulties, Bachrach explains that it is simply how men communicate—a step up from the always popular grunt.

Bachrach believes male nicknames also suggest an intimacy that comes from a secret language known only to the men involved. "Women joke that if you're really a friend, you're on their speed dial. With men, it's more like, 'If I'm really your friend, you have a nickname for me," Bachrach observes.

Paul *Doc*† Leslie, Ph.D. a sociologist at North Carolina's Greens-

*He once hit a woman in the head with a golf ball.
†He has a Ph.D. so students address him as "Doctor."

boro College, has studied nicknames so extensively that he has been guest editor of *Names,* the official journal of the American Name Society. (Motto: "Call us anything you want but just don't call us late for dinner.") Leslie agrees that nicknames are a way of expressing intimacy among men, noting that in doing so they define who's "in" and "out" of the group. "Men use nicknames as boundary markers which create a closeness that excludes those who don't know the nicknames," he comments.

"Nicknames also provide meaning that a given name cannot," Leslie adds, using as an example his old high school friend *Stinky.* Apparently, Stinky was given this pet name by his parents because his diapers were always fuller than the other kids'. It lasted well past infancy. "The more he tried to avoid that nickname as he got older, the more it stayed with him," Leslie notes, laughing.

Leslie has learned that certain groups—especially blues musicians and baseball players—are more likely than others to use nicknames, citing the book *Baseball Nicknames,* by his late colleague James Skipper, Jr. Popular ESPN broadcaster Chris *Boomer** Berman, known for the quirky nicknames he assigns athletes, says baseball monikers date back to an earlier time when games were broadcast over radio and announcers added descriptions to help fans visualize players. Nicknames diminished once games were beamed to home television sets—until Berman signed on with the cable sports network, that is.

"I get letters from old-timers who tell me, 'I don't understand a lot of your rock and roll humor, but I still want to thank you for reviving the lost art of nicknaming,'" Berman notes. The sportscaster has compiled his favorites into *ChrisNames,* an illustrated collection of the more colorful nicknames he offers during baseball and football commentary. His favorites: "John *Tonight Let It Be* Lowenstein" and "Bert *Be Home* Blyleven." My picks: "Julio *Generalissimo* Franco," "Kirk *What Was That* Manwaring," and "Jeff *See Through* Blauser."

Roger *Captain Nemo*† Moeller is a Connecticut archaeologist

---

*His voice is so loud it booms.

†An old computer modem made him sound like he was underwater.

known for the nicknames he assigns anyone who crosses his path. He does this because "there are so few different first names for men," but also because it's fun. "You can pinpoint a personality trait and that person is named forever," Moeller explains.

When he was a graduate student, Moeller met a rather boring fellow named Frank. Frank liked Mickey Mouse. Moeller nicknamed him "Uncle Mickey." Nobody ever called him Frank again. As a bonus, "That nickname transformed his whole personality!" Moeller crows. "You look for a characteristic, and the personality follows."

"When we were younger, it was a way of giving someone grief," agrees Berman, who started nicknaming athletes while drinking beer and reading the box scores with friends. For others, nicknames offer insight into group dynamics, which can help in job situations. Leslie offers a story about a meeting with other academics. One man—we'll call him John Boy—was presenting a controversial proposal and expected Professor James Skipper to support him. At the start of the meeting, John Boy addressed his colleague as *Skip*. As things played out, it became clear that Skip did not endorse the plan. John Boy addressed him next as *Jim*, and by the end of the meeting, when he did not win his battle, he was talking to *Professor Skipper*.

Bachrach shares a story making the rounds in the naming business. Apparently, when the Dallas Cowboys were formed, there was great internal discussion about a nickname. Management didn't want their players known as *Cows*. *Boys* didn't seem right, either. What to do, what to do. The solution was to hire a name consultant clever enough to assign the handle *'Pokes*, short for cowpokes. "It was Southern and it was sexual, but it didn't stick. They're still the *Cowboys*," Bachrach says.

Clever, descriptive nicknames are so irresistible they can get you into trouble—especially the secret ones. I don't think my friend Jane wants her personal trainer, John, to know she calls him *Dirk*, the name she thinks is more appropriate for a trainer. (Plus she likes to say, "Oh no, I can't meet you for lunch today. I'm working out with *Dirk*.") And what about the five-foot-tall appliance repairman identified within one family as *Shortie*—when the youngest slips and calls him Shortie to his face? My favorite from years past got my brother and his friends detention time when they couldn't resist nicknaming their social studies teacher *Master Baden* because of his unusual first name: Baden.

My goal—even though I'm a woman—is to someday acquire a nickname that is as clever as it is descriptive. I want it to be affectionate, but true-to-character. Endearing and enduring. Funny, but not too cute. In my college days, it would have been *Blue Eyes*. Today, it's more likely to be *Wise Guy*.

"MY PROBLEM AND HOW I SOLVED IT"

I work in a male-dominated field. In fact, there's just one other woman in my part of the company. We get tired of the male "approach." The worst example occurred several years ago, before we were so tuned in to sexual harrassment. For my birthday, the guys in the department presented me with an anatomically correct chocolate penis. I was disgusted, but didn't want to give them any pleasure by showing my displeasure.

When the other woman's birthday came around three months later, she and I agreed that I'd invite a male stripper to show up in the office the day before her birthday to preempt any rude activities the men had planned for the next day. The stripper was appropriately lewd, and the men who had initially gathered around out of curiosity were very embarrassed (and probably a little envious).

Since then, all we've received for our birthdays are "Happy Birthday from the Gang" cards. And that's okay with us!

Sally Beth T., Dallas, Texas

TRUE STORY

A man's family was visiting from out of town and he didn't have enough pillowcases for their pillows. Never fear—he slipped the pillows into T-shirts.

STUPID MEN TRICK

Pity the man who thought Downy fabric softener would make his thick, coarse hair softer. It didn't.

WOMEN WANT TO KNOW: INSIGHTS INTO
THE MALE MIND, BY ONE WHO'S BEEN THERE

Why Men Love Sports
by Bill Assimon

Men love sports because sports help them connect with many important things in their lives—with their emotions . . . with family and friends . . . with the past and future.

Gerald Goodman, a psychology professor at UCLA, says men are more comfortable expressing themselves and getting close through some mutual external event or focus—such as a sporting event. This theory might explain why men feel free to express their emotions inside stadiums and in front of television sets, but will not open up anywhere else. It perhaps provides insight into how men can demonstrate physical and verbal affection for their favorite team or player, but not for the women in their lives.

This is why men love sports. Sports allow them to experience so many feelings—excitement, rage, anxiety, hysteria, euphoria—feelings they can't express in other aspects of their lives. All that emotion we exhibit over full-court action is important and real.

Sports offer a language for many men, allowing them to communicate and bond with friends, children, their fathers—or with total strangers. And connection in any form is no small thing. Men relish the sports connections they share with the people in their lives. I know a lot of things may affect my relationships with my friends and family, but I know I will always have sports to share with them.

Sports provide a link that endures, connecting us with pleasant experiences of our past—from playing basketball all day long to celebrating a favorite team's championship. A man can vividly remember the day he got his first baseball glove or the first time he went to a game with his father. This nostalgic bent may explain why he can reel off who won the World Series in 1964, but can't tell you what day he got married.

The magic of sports is that there's always a tomorrow. There's always something to look forward to. No matter what happens, there will always be another game, another season. This promise keeps us going. For a lot of us, a future without sports is no future at all.

Just because sports are such an important part of your man's life doesn't mean you always have to play along. You can love your man but not love the New York Giants. Feigning interest doesn't help, either—it makes men resentful. If you'd rather be outside on a Sunday afternoon than watching a game, then don't hang around.

The key is not necessarily to take part in these sporting rituals but to respect them. Why not allow the men you care about some undiluted pleasure and acknowledge the importance of that in itself? Sounds like a winning strategy to me.*

That magical instrument, the air guitar

Men, and only men, play the air guitar.

In his heart, a man thinks he's cool when he's plucking his magical, musical, mystical air guitar. In her heart, a woman knows her date looks like a dork.

Men defend their silent air concerts. They say they grew up watching a band's lead singer mimic the lead guitarist solo when a young Mick Jagger performed with the Rolling Stones on *The Ed Sullivan Show,* or today, with Whitesnake on MTV. "Every lead singer must grab the microphone, yank the cord, stretch it into a long imaginary guitar, and play along," insists Tony Mathews, a popular morning radio personality in Rochester, New York, who plays his air guitar in the station studio.

Cody Taylor is a Houston camera operator who plays the air guitar to music that is too fast to dance to—the hard-driving stuff. "I hike my leg in the air or do a Pete Townsend thing and twirl around. If it's a blues tune, I bend over a lot," he explains. "I played the air guitar just last night at a club." Did the women flock around? "Well, no, no they didn't," he realizes.

---

*My husband, Bill Assimon, is addicted to college basketball in the worst way, but no intervention is planned.

Computer software technical support specialist Jon Garner of McHenry, Maryland, moonlights as a disc jockey in nightclubs, where his instrument of choice is—of course—the air guitar. "It's another way to express that you're having a good time," he insists. "Since I can't dance when I'm working, I can show I love the music by playing my air guitar."

Freelance disc jockeys have been quick to add the popularity of the air guitar to the bag of tricks they use when entertaining guests at wedding receptions or private parties. One organization in Connecticut tosses cheap inflatable guitars to guests on the dance floor. It's not the women who scramble to grab them and strike up a tune with the records! Air-filled guitars are only a slight improvement over air guitars; move three points up the dork scale.

Radio personality Mathews defends the behavior. "Watch Led Zeppelin's Robert Plant yank and jerk the microphone cord, clutching the mike for all it's worth while stretching out the notes with guitarist Jimmy Page. Those of us in the audience or at home—kept off stage and without benefit of a microphone cord—must make do. We stretch those notes along with Robert or Jimmy, holding nothing but our masculine air guitar," he says. (Is it getting a little warm in here?)

"I can't play a musical instrument but I love music and need to be involved with it," confesses Garner, who prefers to play the air bass guitar, especially to "Radar Love" or a Kiss song. "With the exception of Paul McCartney, bass players are quiet," says Mathews. "They're the underbelly of the band, filling in the bottom with low notes. The bass player barely moves. He stands quiet, confident. The strings on his guitar are the longest, and everybody knows it." (I repeat, is it getting warm in here?)

Taylor remembers a time when he and his young friends saved all their money so they could buy plastic guitars and bash them around someone's basement—just like the real musicians. "It's especially fun when two or more people play the air guitar, or when someone joins in with air drums," he says. What's funnier looking than a man playing the air guitar? A group of them playing air instruments!

Certain types of men are prone to play imaginary instruments, according to Taylor. "They're extroverted—not wallflowers," he explains. "They're easy to approach, someone who doesn't wait to be introduced."

Mathews offers advice to women. "The next time you're in a car, at a party, or just listening to some tunes and a guy suddenly breaks out the air guitar, don't roll your eyes. And don't laugh. Just observe. Or better yet, join in!"

No way. Women are too smart to look so stupid.

"MY PROBLEM AND HOW I SOLVED IT"

In past years, I've spent a lot of time nagging my husband to mow the lawn, one of his few jobs around the house. This summer, I decided to use my time more productively—the energy I spent nagging about the lawn would go elsewhere. For Father's Day, I hired a lawn service to cut the grass on the same day each week. My husband complained about the cost, but I suggested he give it a try and cancel if he felt he could keep up with the grass.

The service stayed with us all summer and the yard always looks lovely.

Valerie T., Northampton, Massachusetts

TRUE STORY

At dinner one night a three-year-old threw up in her plate with no warning. Her mother quickly carried her away to clean her up and do an "illness assessment."

After losing her appetite and settling her daughter in bed, the mother returned to the dining room, assuming her husband and son had either cleaned up the table or taken their plates to the living room to finish eating. Instead, she discovered they had covered the little girl's plate with the table cloth and continued with their meal as if there hadn't been a plateful of barf less than two feet away!

STUPID MEN TRICK

Need clean socks? Stuff them in drinking glasses and run the dishwasher. Wear the socks . . . drink from the glasses.

WOMEN WANT TO KNOW: INSIGHTS INTO
THE MALE MIND, BY ONE WHO'S BEEN THERE

Why Do Men Fish?
by Steve Crane

It comes upon us when we least expect it, like the male equivalent of chocolate craving. There we are, innocently, responsibly, dazedly going about our business when suddenly—*whack!*—we are gripped by a desire that's stronger than hunger, stronger than sex, stronger even than the urge to rip the TV remote out of a woman's hand.

It is the primordial Urge to Catch Fish.

No, this is not the same as the primordial Urge to Relax with Our Feet Up While Sipping Beer in a Bass Boat. That's an entirely different urge, much less powerful and, on the whole, much rarer. Contrary to the perceived wisdom, fishing has nothing whatever to do with relaxing. In fact, it is an intensely aggressive activity. Which is why it is often referred to as the "sport" of fishing.

Real fishermen don't go fishing to relax any more than real boxers open big gashes over each other's eyes because they like the color red. When the Urge comes upon us, there is no earthly power that can distract us from a headlong rush out the door, our phenomenally sensitive fishing rod antennae madly probing the air for the first telltale scent of sunbaked pond scum that signals fish-bearing water.

Nothing can compare with those first few moments when, in a palsied fever of anticipation, your whole body wracked with tremors, you finally succeed in tying a knot and baiting your hook (after professionally testing its sharpness on each of your fingers). Your own blood mixes with that of a cool, brown worm as you air-mail your offering into the boundless mystery beneath your boat.

Ah, ladies, you don't know what you're missing! But it gets better! Because now the real fun begins. Now you . . . *watch the line!*

No two-bit Svengali, no resurrected Rasputin, no brow-beating Ratherian journalist could ever hope to generate the raw psychic wattage of a true fisherman watching his line. At this moment, he is well and truly "plugged in" to the Great Power Source beneath him, feeding it his energy as it, in turn, recharges him.

There may, indeed, be no female equivalent to the electricity that can pass back and forth between a motionless man and a nondescript spot of water over a high-voltage conductor of the thinnest fishing line. But that there is electricity—enough to fry whole blocks of time—cannot be doubted. Thus it is that men can set out at dawn in pursuit of fish, and at dusk look up as if coming out of a trance to ask one another, "Hey, Bubba, you hungry?"*

*Steve Crane's business partner takes credit for introducing him to the joy of fishing.

✈ 5 ✈

Mating
❧ Rituals ❧

✺

If women really understood the dating/mating process, there wouldn't be so many self-help books on the subject. This chapter explores how the evolution of the *Homo slobbius* has shaped the dating experience and influenced the long-term commitment known as marriage. *Warning:* The following information is not for women faint of heart or weak of stomach.

Why don't they call after the first date?

It's a classic. You're parting after the first date. He smiles, revealing the cutest dimples you've ever seen on an adult male. You can't decide what's more mesmerizing—his smile, or those hypnotic blue eyes. He says, "I had a great time. I'll call you."

Of course, he never does. It's enough to make you join a convent.

Why do men do this? Why say, "I'll call," if you have no intention of doing so? Why not just say, "I had a nice evening. Good night."?

I asked many fellows across the country to explain this behavior. Their observations are honest and shocking, reminding us that men and women view intimacy quite differently.

Men don't call again because they don't want a second date. But why say "I'll call" when you know you won't? Because, many said, they "don't want to hurt the woman's feelings." Logic suggests that not saying anything at all would be less humiliating and painful than saying you'll be in touch, leaving the woman waiting breathlessly for the next opportunity to hear once again about your hemorrhoid surgery.

One refreshingly straightforward man explained why a second date isn't always appealing. "We men want only one thing, and if we can't get it on the first date, we'll dump you." Another verified this theory, which left me confused. Hmm . . . let's see. . . . you don't like her enough to go on a second date, but you like her enough to sleep with her on the first date. Talk about male logic.

And having "gone that far," isn't she even more likely to expect you to call after the first date? Well, yes, says one man. "I handle that by rating her on the 'Alex Scale,'" he explains. (Alex was the Glenn Close character in *Fatal Attraction,* the movie that had every man in America buying flowers for his wife.) "I determine how much of a psycho she is, then decide if I can wean her away, or just not call at all." Generally, they tell us, men who don't call after an intimate evening have moved on to the next challenge. The hunt is over. Time to find new prey.

On occasion, we run into these yo-yos again. The braver gals among us challenge them, asking, "So why didn't you call? You said you would!" Most of them don't even stumble or stammer when confronted. This has happened before, and they have a response. Explanations offered most frequently are:

1. "I lost your number."
2. "I got back together with my old girlfriend."
3. "I didn't want to hurt your feelings."
4. "I washed those pants and the paper with your number disintegrated." (Usually used with women whom men are ambivalent about—maybe they want to see you again; maybe not.)
5. "I was called away on a CIA mission. I could tell you about it—but then I'd have to kill you."
6. "I dropped dead from yellow fever."

Ladies, spare yourself this humiliation. Identify losers—and users—sooner. Study their body language and how they're communicating with you. Look out for the fellow who pays little attention to what you're saying because his eyes are constantly surveying the restaurant for his next conquest. At the other extreme, beware the man who tells you within the first hour of your first date that:

- You are the most [insert your favorite adjective here] woman he has ever met.
- He never thought he would fall in love—until now.
- He wonders if you believe in love at first sight.
- You would make a great mother.

The most extreme users know your hot buttons and keep score as they try to see how many they can hit in one evening. That's not to say that every man who says on the first date that he can see himself married to you is insincere, but there's a good chance that he's full of it.

Once you've learned to identify a man who isn't good enough for you, cut your losses quickly. When he takes you home and says with that charming smile, "I had a great time. I'll call," respond, "Don't bother."

He won't.

WARNING LINES

Judith Newman, author of *Tell Me Another One: A Woman's Guide to Classic Men's Lines,* is adept at spotting losers as soon as they open their mouths. Here are a few of her favorite warning lines:

- "You remind me so much of my mother!"
- "I'm a rebel."
- "A lot of mistakes are made in the name of loneliness." (Usually the rationale of a man cheating on his wife.)

- "You know, I only date gorgeous women." (Often spoken by a man wearing a toupee and pinkie ring.)
- "I'm haunted by my potential."
- "But that's just another part of me you'll learn to love." (Refers to a particularly horrifying habit—and he probably has many.)

"MY PROBLEM AND HOW I SOLVED IT"

I was being pursued by a man I had dated a few times, but ultimately was not attracted to. It seemed as if he was always in my face—at my doorstep, or in the same nightspot on a Saturday night. He was not shy about making his presence known, and it became annoying very quickly, especially because it looked to other men as if we were a "couple" and I was unavailable.

I finally enlisted the help of an old friend I ran into one night in a bar. When the obnoxious fellow showed up—as predicted—my old friend "bumped into" me and pretended he was my long lost elementary school playmate. He elbowed the other guy out of position and began reminiscing about the good old days—all fiction, but done quite convincingly. The other guy took the hint and disappeared for good. I realized then that all he needed to see was that he had competition—apparently, he couldn't accept that being with nobody was better than being with him!

Theresa S., Cortland, New York

TRUE STORY

A national survey reveals that almost two-thirds of the women questioned admit that someone persuaded them to sleep with him (or her) by successfully lying. Forty-two percent of the deceived women say they suffered long-term damage. The lie the majority of the partners used to get the woman into bed? "I love you."

STUPID MEN TRICK

Whoa—you've got a hot date and need to impress her with a shirt and jacket. But you're in a hurry. Iron just the front of the shirt, and don't take the jacket off.

Want to see my dentures?
Why older men date younger women

What could a middle-aged man see in a perky twenty-five-year-old who has never altered her svelte body with a pregnancy? What could possibly be appealing about someone who hasn't even imagined everything an older man has already experienced? What is the point of dating nymphets who ask you to pick up a tube of Clearasil on your way over? What could an older man and a younger woman possibly have in common, beyond Tony Bennett?

You probably know at least one older man who would jump at the chance to date a younger woman. Yet, as an "older" woman, you get nauseous thinking of dating a twenty-ish fellow. You've always been attracted to older men. Research shows women place less emphasis on appearance, preferring instead maturity and experience. Men, victims of their own testosterone, can't get past a young and pretty face. As R. Don Steele explains in *How to Date Young Women for Men Over 35,* "Stuff what they say about beauty only being skin deep. Fat bellies, saggy breasts, stretch marks and wide asses are not attractive."

Them's fightin' words.

Steele, fifty-four, has been dating younger women for more than two decades because, "They are so much more fun! They have more of the qualities men like—sweetness, kindness, niceness, mothering, and nurturing."

Why is that, oh Don of the Nubile?

"Around 35, women start to get hostile toward men because of the damage men have done to them. These women have so much emotional baggage to carry around," he explains.

Guy Zipp, thirty-nine, agrees. He dates younger women because women his own age "usually have a lot more mental scars, negative attitudes, and baggage," he notes. A Buffalo, New York, aerospace engineer, Zipp is dating a twenty-four-year-old who respects his knowledge and experience.

David Buss, Ph.D., a psychology professor at the University of Michigan and author of *The Evolution of Desire,* believes older men are compelled to fawn over younger women for evolutionary reasons. He says men today, like their Neanderthal predecessors, are still attracted to women of childbearing age, even though there isn't the same need to breed to perpetuate the species anymore. "The male standards of attraction are based on cues to youth and cues to health, because these are indicators of fertility. These include clear, unwrinkled skin; full lips; and symmetrical features," he observes.

Buss compares human mating to that of chimps, explaining that the female chimp has visible, physical signs that she is ovulating and can conceive. When the male chimp sees these signs, he knows it's time to reproduce the species. Human females do not offer these visible fertility cues. All a man knows is that younger women are more fertile than older women. So he makes his decision about her potential as a breeder based on physical signs of youth.

Marriage counselor Norman Goldner, Ph.D., who co-wrote *Why Women and Men Don't Get Along* with his wife, Carol Rhodes, agrees, explaining that men are following their biological programming to continue their genetic material. Apparently, these men are mindless androids, executing commands flashed to them by their DNA, without regard for whether they have children already or not, or whether the world would be a better place if they continued—or discontinued—their genetic material.

Raul Field,* thirty-nine, a Chicago law enforcement officer, knows nothing of such academic theories. Instead, Field says he prefers younger women for "typical guy reasons—younger women are more attractive than older women." Younger women appreciate Field, he says, because he's "a nice guy: I don't hit, I don't drink, I don't lie."

The complicated lives of older women also make them less attractive to some fellows. "If she's got children, you have to get along with her kids, too," complains Field. "I dated one nice woman whose son reminded me of Pugsley Adams. What was I

*Not his real name.

supposed to tell her? I like you, but I can't stand your son? Then there's the kid's father, if he's still involved. That's worse."

Author/"expert" Steele believes his own interest in the younger babe has something to do with his "inner child." "She's an emotional peer to the guy inside who never grew up," he explains, noting that his own inner self has been twenty-seven for some time. Then there's the need to fix mistakes. "He wants to go back and do it all over again and get it right this time," Steele adds.

Fortunately for us older gals, these exceptional specimens will consider dating women closer to their own age, especially those who take care of themselves. But Steele isn't very encouraging, citing reports that 75 percent of men who remarry select a woman at least ten years younger. He says there's not much hope for us, suggesting instead that we raise our daughters differently.

"Teach your daughter to work for a living so she won't be dependent on any man, and tell her to wait until she's thirty to get married. Today's typical woman could be divorced at twenty-eight with two children and no job skills, and you don't want that to happen to your daughters," Steele insists.

So what are the options for the thirty-five-plus single woman? Our experts offer advice: Zipp suggests working at being spontaneous and staying young. Chicago's Field advises, "Quit smoking, drinking, and wearing makeup, and join a health club."

And remember, when it comes to advice, you get what you pay for.

"MY PROBLEM AND HOW I SOLVED IT"

This chain letter was started by a woman like you hoping to bring relief to other tired and discontented women. Unlike most chain letters, this one does not cost anything. Just send a copy to five of your friends who are equally frustrated. Then, bundle up your husband or boyfriend, send him to the woman whose name appears at the top of the list, and add yours to the bottom.

When your name comes to the top, you will receive 16,877 men ... one of them is bound to be a hell of a lot better than the one you already have. *Do not break the chain.* One woman did and got her own SOB back. At this writing, a friend of mine already received

184 men. They buried her yesterday, but it took three undertakers 36 hours to get the smile off her face.

Send this along quickly so my name moves up!

(Several copies of this letter came across the author's fax machine.)

TRUE STORY

A researcher at New York City's Museum of Natural History has discovered that male cockroaches stay out later than female cockroaches.

STUPID MEN TRICK

Don't you hate it when your mustache is too gray? Darken it with a black Magic Marker and watch the young chicks flock to your side.

For better or for worse:
Why men marry

The groom's shoes said it all. A mischievous friend had painted words on the bottom of them. As the husband-to-be knelt at the altar with the soles of his shoes exposed to the congregation, bold letters implored, "H-E-L-P M-E!" It was funny—and I laughed—but it also was symbolic. Common folklore is that marriage is practically a death sentence for men, but the start of a wonderfully fulfilling new life for women.

Guess again.

Current research—disputed, of course—reveals that men in fact fare *better* in marriages. *USA Today* quotes University of Washington psychologist Neil Jacobsen in *Family Therapy News* on his research into women, depression, and marital therapy: "If you want a recipe for depression, have a woman get married and have young children. If you want a recipe for male well-being, have him do the same," Jacobson said. His colleague, psychologist John Gottman, wrote in a recent study, "There is substantial evidence marriage disproportionately benefits men. At all ages, husbands report higher levels of marital satisfaction than do wives."

Looks like the shoes were on the wrong feet.

So if men are actually happier when they're married than when they are single, why is it so hard to get some of them to say "I do"?

One expert on bachelors says it's because some men really, really like their freedom. Charles Waehler, Ph.D., assistant professor of psychology at the University of Akron in Ohio, studies longtime bachelors, classifying them as flexible, rigid, or ambivalent.

Flexible bachelors date and establish relationships. They can be close to a woman, but can also pull away. Rigid bachelors have difficulty relating to others, feel inferior in the company of women, and have little interest in interacting with others. They keep the world at arm's length. Ambivalent bachelors are confused—one minute they want to be involved, the next minute they don't. "Ambivalent bachelors drive women crazy," Waehler observes. He notes that while the three types exhibit different attitudes toward marriage, they all value self-reliance and enjoy being independent of others.

Waehler believes these committed bachelors, as well as other single men, are most likely to decide to get married when something happens to change the course of their lives—completing a degree, transferring to a new location, losing both parents. Once change is in motion, it's easier to include the adjustments introduced by marriage, he observes.

Another theory suggests it's also likely that one day a man wakes up disgusted by the pig sty he calls home and admits it's time to get a live-in maid. Married men truly enjoy sharing stories of the filth they tolerated when surviving as happy-go-lucky single fellows. The fungus in the shower and piles of odiferous laundry disappeared when they committed to "the little woman" and—lo and behold!—friends started staying long enough to use the bathroom. (There is no scientific evidence to support this theory of male marriage motivation; research is purely anecdotal.)

Anthropologist Richard Schweder of the University of Chicago is one who believes men get married when they're ready to have children. "If the issue of having children didn't arise, people probably wouldn't get married," he observes. Schweder's work with communities in India reinforces this belief. "When I pose to Indians the hypothetical question, 'What do you think of a married couple who decides not to have children?', they look at me and say, 'Why did they ever get married?' It is incomprehensible to them that someone would get married and choose to not have children. Because the point of marriage is reproduction of legitimate heirs," he explains.

Greg Godek, author of *1001 Ways to Be Romantic,* adds that while a man might tell you he's not interested in being married, something could happen to change his mind quickly. "One day he's a confirmed bachelor and the next day he's ready to get married because he's found the 'right' woman," Godek explains. "It hits us like a ton of bricks because our emotions are two levels below our conscious state." (Translation: "One day he's a confirmed bachelor, and the next day, he discovers he's tired of picking up dinner at McDonald's every night. *Voilà!* He falls in love with the first woman he meets who can cook!")

Charlotte Richards believes a man just has to be ready for marriage. Richards owns five wedding chapels in Las Vegas and has performed nearly half a million wedding ceremonies during the past thirty-five years. "Most men should marry the woman they can't live without, not the woman they could live *with!*" she says.

But Godek warns men against "making a lifelong decision based on hormones." He advises them to use his "60 percent plus spark" formula. "You can't get 100 percent of what you're looking for in one person, so you have to decide what you'll settle for. Usually, 60 percent and the spark from the right chemistry are enough for most people." (Godek admits that in his marriage, "it's more like 75 to 80 percent plus spark.")

Psychologist Waehler's research with longtime bachelors suggests they are a particularly tough nut to crack. He suggests that women in these relationships examine their own motives for wanting to marry men who have been single so long. Does she truly want to marry *him* because she's in love with him, or does she want to marry him so she can prove she's woman enough to convert him, he wonders.

The best way to strengthen a relationship with a very independent single man, Waehler suggests, is to foster your own sense of self. "Express how important your independence is to you, and you'll be more attractive to him," he explains. Show, don't tell. Saying "Gosh, I really like being home alone on a Saturday night" isn't enough. Instead, make plans with other friends on the weekend so he has an appreciation for what it's like to be single on date night.

Waehler's couples-counseling experience suggests that one of the best ways to encourage a lifetime commitment from a man is to do things he likes to do with him. Get two remote controls. (Just kidding.) "A man communicates by doing things. A woman wants to pull him into her verbal world, but going the other way and doing, rather than saying, will actually endear her to him," Waehler says.

But your interest in his activities must be sincere. Otherwise, he will begin to see you as an anchor holding him back. If you view football as the ultimate expression of foolish male aggression, tagging along to a game is not a good idea, even if you've brought a good book. If your idea of roughing it is a Motel 6, you should skip the backpacking excursion planned for next weekend. But you might enjoy motorcycling, fishing, or sitting on the front steps drinking beer and spitting watermelon seeds.

Still, don't expect him to do the same for you. The shoes that say H-E-L-P *M-E!* are on *his* feet, remember?

"MY PROBLEM AND HOW I SOLVED IT"

I have always avoided being unkind to men I don't want to date. I don't like to hurt feelings. Still, I didn't know what to do about the man who had trouble accepting "No thank you" for an answer. No matter how many times I turned down his offers, he kept calling. Finally, my roommate came up with the solution. She answered the telephone every time it rang. Eventually, this guy called, and she told him I had married unexpectedly and moved out of state. He stopped calling.

Pauline D., Salem, Oregon

TRUE STORY

One male college student was smarter than he looked. Like most everybody, he hated doing laundry, but unlike the rest of us, he figured out how to get clean clothes without paying for a service.

He'd go to the laundromat, put his dirty clothes in the *dryer,* then begin adding powdered detergent. Without a doubt, someone—usually a female—would stop him. He'd play dumb, and she'd wash, dry, and fold his laundry for him. He has done this many times, and it always worked.

STUPID MEN TRICK

Avoid using the dishwasher, especially when the "little woman" isn't home. Clean your dishes by pouring dishwasher detergent over them after setting them out in the rain. To dry those rain-washed dishes, put them in the microwave.

✦ 6 ✦

There's No Cave
✌ like Home ✌

∽◦∾

Is a man's home his castle? That depends on whether a castle is supposed to need (1) its gutters cleaned out and its lightbulbs replaced; (2) an electronic device that helps fellows locate mysteriously disappearing car keys, sunglasses, and bottle openers; and (3) a sick ward for men only.

"Where are my car keys?"
Why men can't find things that are
right under their noses

Is the female uterus equipped with a built-in homing device? Or are women born with an extra gene that helps them find things that are right under a man's nose?

Actually, reports geneticist Jane Gitschier, Ph.D., associate professor of medicine and pediatrics at the University of California, San Francisco, women would not have an extra gene. It's more likely that there's a suppressor gene in man that impedes his ability to find things. "It's much like the suppressor on the gene for shopping," she says.

Women *must* have something hardwired into them to help them find things men can't see—car keys, brown belts, bottle openers, butter in the refrigerator. Otherwise, why would a man always ask the nearest female where the missing object might be? In reality, the brown belt is right where he left it—under his nose, practically—but he just can't seem to find it. Folklore has it that even Albert Einstein had these problems. One story says that his housekeeper would lead him by the hand to his office because he never bothered to learn how to get from his home to his job. It's a luxury only a man could afford.

The leaders of the men's movement will no doubt debate that men have more trouble finding things than women, or that men turn to women to help them unearth their worldly goods. Yet any secretary or wife with more than six weeks on the job will tell you that men rely heavily on women to keep track of everything from top-secret documents to nail clippers. Likewise, most women could tell you that if you put things in the same place each time, you'll eventually teach yourself where to find those things. But that requires common sense (see Chapter 9).

Sociologist Charlie Case of Augusta College in Georgia explains the situation: "We guys have momentous thoughts on our minds—we're so consumed with such heavy important worldly things that keeping track of our keys or our wallets or what day of the week it is, is just too mundane for us."

A common theory shared by psychology professor Don Nance of Wichita State University is that, "Men historically hunted and brought the food back. Then it was up to the women to do everything else with it—clean it, prepare it, and make clothes out of it. Men historically have not paid as much attention to maintenance at home and that's why once I'm done driving the car, I put the keys down and I'm not concerned about where they are until I need them again." Of course not. He can just ask his wife where he put them.

After all, that has always been the woman's job, reminds Chris Kilmartin, instructor of "The Psychology of Men" at Mary Washington College in Fredericksburg, Virginia. "The home has long been defined as the woman's sphere and domain, so the woman organizes the home," he explains. Kilmartin suggests it is not macho to be on top of things at home. "Males are raised to avoid being feminine. It is feminine to be aware of household details, and being feminine is a threat to a man's masculinity. Many men act incompetent on purpose because to be competent in the house is to be feminine," he notes. Now here's a man who knows what he's talking about.

Case, the Georgia sociologist, also believes it has a lot to do with control and masculinity. "Men are supposed to be in charge and in control, and when they can't master little things like finding their wallet or where they've parked their car, it is very frustrating. A man is likely to go into a state of great agitation when his frailty as a human being is so starkly exposed," Case says. Ironically, he is exposed because he chooses not to find things. Case says that's because *it's not his job to find things.* "The mundane details of survival and day-to-day maintenance are woman's work. The man is able to pass them off first to his mother, then to his girlfriend, then on to his wife."

Malcolm Kushner, a California attorney turned humor consultant, believes it depends on what he's looking for. "I, for example, can't find dirty dishes in the sink because I don't like to do that sort of thing," he observes with candor.

A social worker at a psychiatric hospital in Norman, Oklahoma, Paul Somerville, offers other theories explaining this male forgetfulness:

- Men are idiots who are lucky if they find their way home at night.
- Men are brilliant but evil creatures who spend so much time thinking up ways to bedevil women that they find it hard to remember things such as where they put their car keys.
- Men are so preoccupied with sex that they can never remember any of the details of day-to-day life. It is only when men are involved in relationships with women who make remembering these things a prerequisite for sex that men are able to remember such details at all.

- Men are pining for the Lost Warrior within, grieving for the primitive spirit which lives inside them yet dares not express itself. They are too distracted by their grief to remember anything.

Nose expert Alan Hirsch, M.D., director of the Smell & Taste Treatment and Research Foundation in Chicago, believes it's much simpler than that. "I see it as a transference down from our mothers, who always know where everything is—they're omniscent," he says with the reverence due mothers.

What these experts are reluctant to say point-blank, however, is that women participate in this grown-up game of hide and seek. Men ask us where something is; we tell them. As psychologist Nance explains it, "The interesting thing is that men are much more that way when women are around. In other words, we really rely on you. If you're not there to do it—lo and behold!—we discover these untapped abilities for organizing and for finding keys and brown belts and shoes—even what clothes to wear!"

"In the home, a man can get all of his dependencies taken care of," adds Kilmartin.

Nance and Kilmartin recommend that women not play the game, deferring the inquiries with neutral comments such as, "I don't use your sneakers so I don't know where they are," or "You might try looking where you put them."

Case, reflecting the sense of humor required of someone who studies human behavior, is even more practical. "I like the approach used when we were children, when our mittens were tied together. Maybe you could tie his gloves to his beer cooler or his car keys to his TV remote," he suggests.

That solution strikes a chord with Somerville, who declares, "Why is it that men, who can never find the car keys even when they're right under their noses, never, ever lose track of the TV remote control? Huh?"

Because regardless of their differences, men still share the X chromosome with women. This must be how they get in touch with their more feminine side.

"My Problem and How I Solved It"

My husband had this irritating way of draping his neckties over the stair bannister every night after work. I didn't like looking at them, so for a long time, I put them away in his closet. But I really didn't enjoy picking up after him. So I began letting them collect on the railing, like holiday garlands.

Eventually, we had a nice arrangement draped ever so gracefully. When a friend came to visit one evening, she commented on the necktie arrangement and asked if it was a new trend in home decorating.

For whatever reason, my husband was mortified. (You'd think we were talking about his undershorts!) He has since stopped decorating the house with his accessories.

Lucy G., Toronto, Ontario

True Story

Here's a reality check: Roper Starch Worldwide compared results of surveys conducted in 1946 and 1993 to learn that fewer men today think women have "the easier time in present-day America." In 1946, 46 percent of the men surveyed thought women had it easier than men. That number decreased to just 22 percent in the later survey.

Stupid Men Trick

Don't worry about lead poisoning—go ahead and stir your coffee with a pencil.

WOMEN WANT TO KNOW: INSIGHTS INTO
THE MALE MIND, BY ONE WHO'S BEEN THERE.

Male Time Dysfunction, or Why It Takes
Two Weeks to Change a Lightbulb
by Tom Powell

Why does it take two weeks to change a lightbulb? It relates to a condition recognized among sociologists as male time dysfunction. Allow me to explain. Most of us fellows save our household tasks for the weekend. Coincidentally, many religions of the world observe Saturday or Sunday as a day of rest. Men want to respect that observance faithfully. To be on the safe side, we honor both days.

There are other logical and reasonable answers to why men's time schedules are different from women's. Consider genetics and social conditioning. Guys suffer from random, chaotic, and irregular Pre-Testosterone Syndrome (PTS). We can treat, or prevent, the discomfort associated with PTS by vegetating in front of a TV. Simultaneously exercising the arms and elbows, as when drinking beer, also helps.

In addition, findings from one research project show that after age thirty, men lose their hearing twice as fast as women. Thus, men are not ignoring women; they just do not hear them. Another study found that males don't attempt or complete chores because of an obsession with planning. Which means they never get to it.

It's a shame that, on a typical weekend, a man will not voluntarily submit to performing a few tasks and errands—landscaping the yard; painting the house inside and out; checking out sales at twenty-three stores; shopping for new carpet, wallpaper, and appliances before buying a month's groceries on the way home; and so on.

If male time dysfunction has become an issue in your household, try these behavior modification techniques proven effective:

1. Hide the remote control.
2. Buy your partner hearing aids.
3. Inform him you are related to Lorena Bobbitt and may have inherited some of her behavior characteristics.
4. Before expressing your interest in wallpapering the kitchen, read aloud an article containing the Surgeon General's warning that lead-based paint causes impotency, sterility, and baldness.
5. Show your partner the red tag in the garage left by the city code enforcement inspector warning that the house will be condemned on Monday if the boxes are not neatly stacked

and the floor swept in accordance with municipal ordinances pertaining to aesthetics and ecology.

6. Threaten to withhold the *S* word (supper).
7. Call your mother and invite her to stay at least a month so she can help you with chores.

I'd offer more tips, but I've got to watch a baseball game while I figure out why I shouldn't fix the lock on the apartment door.*

Do sick men make women sick?

"Anything a woman has, a man has worse," declares writer Margo Kaufman on the subject of sick men. "They have this ability to magnify the smallest incident and illness. For example, if a woman has a cold, she goes to work, takes care of her kids, takes care of her husband, does whatever she has to do, and takes a Contac. That's it. But with a man it's an opportunity to revert to childhood. He immediately lets you know that life has stopped."

Kaufman represents current female thinking that sick men are much, much sicker than sick women. For the most part, it is what university types refer to as "common lore"—we are generalizing based on what we've seen, but there probably isn't any hard research proving that men whine more than women when they have the common cold.

What *is* proven, however, is that women go to the doctor's office more often, but men are actually *hospitalized* more frequently. Sherrie Kaplan, M.D., a researcher at the Health Institute of the New England Medical Center in Boston, says researchers are not sure if men ignore the symptoms until the problem is so severe it requires hospitalization, or if men just have "more major stuff going on."

Michael Lafavore, editor of *Men's Health,* describes it as "that walking wounded thing. Guys tend to put off dealing with their

*Tom Powell has been single for ten years and misses procrastinating on weekends.

illness until they can't function anymore," he explains. "You had better be *really* sick if you're not out there doing those manly things," concurs Michael Fleming, M.D., a family physician in Shreveport, Louisiana.

Lafavore adds that men complain so much because it doesn't feel right to be sick. "Most of the guys around my age were told to tough it out, keep a stiff upper lip, and don't let it get you down. If you're hurt at football practice, you're supposed to just walk it off. In the movies we watched, when John Wayne got an arrow in his leg, he took a slug of whiskey and pulled the arrow out himself before going on with the rest of his adventure. The message we got was that it's not manly to be sick, so we have a really hard time dealing with it," he observes.

Researcher Kaplan notes, "The way we teach men how to behave in respect to their health care is a little dysfunctional. We probably do socialize them to walk it off and not attend to their health. And once they get to a doctor, we don't teach them that it's okay to be concerned about their health and to ask and get information. We don't teach them that asking questions of a physician does not mean the man is weak, simple, or stupid."

Lafavore believes that if men seem more uncomfortable with aches and pains, it's for an unexpected reason. "What makes guys miserable is being home during the daytime," explains Lafavore. "It's a woman's world. You've got *Oprah* and *All My Children* on. It doesn't feel right to be home and that makes us feel even worse." It's certainly not because the pain gets to them, Lafavore is quick to point out. "I don't think men are big babies and can't stand pain," he asserts.

Fleming, the family physician, disagrees, conceding that men don't deal well with pain and discomfort. "Women are more stoic," he says. "When men get sick, we want our mothers. We want to be nurtured."

Well, you're out of luck. According to Lafavore, "No one has time for sympathy anymore. Maybe when Dad was sick in the fifties, Mom would bring him some chicken soup and ginger ale, but Mom works now and she doesn't have time. She's got kid problems, and day-care problems, and work problems."

Or is it more complicated than that? Is the pampering insufficient because women of the nineties have so many more demands on their time, or is there another insidious reason why women don't fuss over sick men the way men want women to?

"I sense from women that they have a really hard time with the idea of their male companion being sick. Women don't like it when their man is laid low or weak, anymore than men do," Lafavore comments. An article in Lafavore's magazine by Denis Boyles explains that women are afraid that a sick man "might not be able to care for her—in sickness or otherwise. If you get sick, you may be putting her long-term care at risk."

Puh-leeze! Who do they think they're kidding?

Kaufman, author of *1-800-AM-I-NUTS?,* says that, in reality, men whine and whimper at the first sign of a runny nose because they know a woman will respond. "It's cute for about half an hour," she notes. "Then it's like they're on vacation. They act in a shameless way, as if all the rules have been thrown away."

Men also find it difficult to rally when roles are reversed and the female in the relationship is incoherent from fever and pain. Smart women don't expect much care beyond the bare minimum when they're ill—usually a trip to the drugstore at best—because most men don't know how to nurture. Smart women, too, prevent unnecessary health problems. Researcher Kaplan believes that women are better at taking care of themselves because they are usually responsible for the family's health as well. "Women are the ones who take the children to the doctor's, take themselves to the doctor for reproductive care, and who oftentimes accompany a sick partner to the doctor," says Kaplan.

Actually, it's more likely that she *dragged* him to the doctor's. As physician Fleming points out, "Men don't want to see a doctor. It's a sign that they're not feeling well, and therefore not capable." With this in mind, it's probably not such a bad idea to pamper the dears at the first sign of sprain or strain. A little TLC at the onset might be the best preventive medicine available—even if it's generic TLC.

But beware the guy who sees this as an opportunity to take an indefinite leave of absence from reality. If he abuses the situation and expects a nursemaid to go beyond her tolerance level (six to twenty-four hours), turn the tables: Get sick yourself. Snookems will head back to work so fast he won't have time to serve you lukewarm tea and burnt toast. But maybe he'll toss you the TV remote.

SHE'S SICK, HE'S SICK

Here's what women—and men—say when they're not feeling well:

She Says	*He Says*
My nose is a little runny.	I'm allergic to my job!
I have a sore throat.	Do I still have tonsils?
I'm a little achy. I wonder if I'm catching that flu going around.	Do you have the phone number for the ambulance?
Ow! I just hit my thumb with the hammer! I need ice.	*Ow!* I just hit my thumb with the hammer! Call 911!
Uh-oh. I think I sprained my ankle.	Can you drive me to the emergency room?
I have a headache.	Did you know there's a history of brain tumors in my family?
My nose got sunburned.	What do third-degree burns look like?
I hope this antibiotic kicks in soon.	Do I have disability insurance?
Have you ever noticed this mole before?	I've got skin cancer!

SAD FACTS ABOUT SICK MEN

Men generally are less likely than women to discuss health problems with their physicians. Other key facts about men and health:

- Male physicians spend an average of five minutes less with each patient than do female physicians.
- Men are less inclined than women to ask for more information about prescription medicines.
- Men are more likely to ask questions of a female physician than of a male doctor.
- Male physicians spend less time with male patients, give them less information, and use more technical language than they do with female patients.
- Fewer men (72%) than women (86%) visit a doctor each year.
- One in four men with symptoms of sexual dysfunction or depression discuss the problem with a doctor.
- Men have seven times as many cases of hospitalization due to emotional breakdowns related to breakups with girl-friends or wives.

"MY PROBLEM AND HOW I SOLVED IT"

My husband is responsible for taking out the kitchen garbage in our apartment. For whatever reason, he lets it pile practically to the ceiling before he'll take out the old bag and put in the new one. By then, it's almost impossible to fit the mound of trash into the bag.

It didn't take me long to start buying extra large trash bags. Now, when he *finally* takes the bag out, all he has to do is pull the extra plastic over the top of the mountain and tie it up.

Mary Kay S., Dallas, Texas

TRUE STORY

When my husband was too sick to go to work, he stretched out on the couch and watched TV all day—until it broke. "Honey," he called, "the television is broken." "Don't worry, I'll call a repairman later. Take a nap," I replied from the kitchen.

"Honey!" he hollered again forty-five minutes later. "When's the repairman coming?" "By the end of the week," I told him. "By the end of the week?" he repeated, incredulous. "I can't last that long!"

He put on his shoes and coat, grabbed the car keys, and said,

"Come on. We're going to buy a new television set." We did—right then and there. We brought it home, then he dragged it inside, set it up, turned it on, and collapsed back on the couch.

"I'm so *siiiiiiick,*" he moaned.

Stupid Men Trick

After prostate surgery, you have occasional bleeding when urinating. Geez, you hate to see that blood. Doc says you can ignore it, or he'll fix it. Instead of doing either, you pee in the concrete laundry tub so you won't see the blood.

✦ 7 ✦

Reproducing the
❧ Species ❧

❧❧❧

Is it true that if men gave birth, the population of the world would drop significantly? Let's review the transformation of the *Homo slobbius* into a parent.

Why men have children

With more mothers in the workforce, the marriage license no longer guarantees a built-in nanny. That's why so many fellows have become more contemplative about why they have children and how many they can handle and support.

One study reports that men with wives who work outside the home have smaller families than men whose wives stay home. Is this because the women resist raising larger families while pursuing careers—or because the men are forced to be more involved with childcare and become overwhelmed? One can't help but wonder if men would have fewer children—like just the first one—if they were the ones to stay home with their children all day, every day, seven days a week.

Jerrold Lee Shapiro, Ph.D., author of *The Measure of a Man: Becoming the Father You Wish Your Father Had Been,* says there are many reasons why men have children, some related to ethnicity or social class. Underneath it all, there is an "innate reproductive need," he says. "They want to be fathers to pass things on to the next generation."

"It really is a continuation of biology. It's immortality," agrees Arthur Dobrin, Ph.D., a Long Island family therapist. This is especially true for middle-class men, whose work is more abstract, than for construction workers, who can see the results of their labor when they've finished a job. "If you're an office worker and you work on a computer, what do you have to show for it? The way in which these men are able to leave something behind is through their children," Dobrin explains.

This egotistical "leave something behind" concept is difficult for women to understand, which explains why so few name their children after themselves. "The motivations among men and women are different," agrees Dobrin. "Women are much more relationally oriented, and children present another form of relationships." For some women, having children provides the opportunity to eat animal crackers or a legitimate excuse for going to Disney movies. But for men, it's a manly man who can prove his virility with offspring.

"For some, having children proves you have sperm, and having more children proves you have more sperm," comments Thomas Blume, Ph.D., a family therapist in Birmingham, Michigan. Blume cites situations when this has motivated men to badger women into having more children than the women want. Experts say this motivation is more common among younger men who feel they have something to prove.

Interestingly, other men become fathers almost automatically. "In some cases, men don't even think about it—it's an assumption that's never been questioned," explains Tom Gerschick, a sociologist at Illinois State University who lectures on men and masculinity topics. "With others, especially those with higher incomes, they are so ambivalent they don't even make a decision—they hope for birth control failure so the decision will be made for them." These are most likely the men who introduce their youngest as their "Oopsie Baby," not exactly an esteem builder.

The more tender souls, Shapiro notes, have offspring because children provide an opportunity to be openly affectionate. It's not manly to be mushy with your buddies or pals, but you can hug and kiss your kids all you want. Still others, he says, want to pass along what they've learned in life, and they do this through their children. Only a man would say he has children so he can share his knowledge with the world.

Blume adds that, for some, a child is a chance to relive your life and correct your mistakes. A motivation for many, says Shapiro, is the opportunity to be the father you wish your own father had been. If this is your reason, Shapiro notes, you must evaluate what you didn't like in your own upbringing and work very hard not to do things the same way. This is difficult because so much of what we do or say as parents is automatic—such as repeating phrases our parents used with us: "Because I said so!" "Turn off that noise!" "You'll go blind if you keep doing that!"

"Figuring out what they need to learn from their own dads is so crucial in terms of changing the way men parent. For men, in some ways, there's a real opening to do that because of all the advances we've got from the women's movement and the possibility to be much more involved with our kids," Shapiro adds.

Whether men have children and the number they have is often tied to their social class and ethnic background. While Gerschick notes that he is unaware of any studies of birth rate by socioeconomic level—meaning actual proof that yuppies have fewer children than the middle-class folks—he believes that there is a stereotype of working-class people as being strongly identified with their families. These are the men who will think the least about whether to have children, and are more likely to have larger families—if stereotypes hold true.

These are the men who go through life just knowing they will have children without being terribly introspective. Add to that category National Public Radio commentator Bob Garfield, who tries not to be too philosophical about such matters. His reason for having children? "Five words: 'Honey, get daddy a beer.' "

"IF IT'S A BOY, WE CAN NAME HIM AFTER ME!"

Women do not feel compelled to name their daughters after themselves in the same ways that men do. Edwin Lawson, Ph.D., of Fredonia, New York, an officer of the American Name Society and an expert on names in general, knows why that is. "It has a hell of a lot to do with ego and vanity," he says with conviction. "He had a kid on an ego kick. His attitude is 'it's my house, my yacht, my wife, and my kid.' "

Long Island family therapist Arthur Dobrin compares the "junior" syndrome to the monuments men have built to themselves. "When the father is gone, Junior or Tony or George is literally still there with that very name."

Some interesting facts about "juniors," as they are known among members of the American Name Society:

- Nineteen percent of male children are named after their fathers.
- Children named for their fathers are more likely to be abused than those who aren't.
- "Juniors" are three times as likely as nonjuniors to have mental illness.
- Fewer people seem to be attaching the abbreviation "Jr." to the name, although 38 percent of the women surveyed on this subject by a diaper service said they are naming their children after a relative—usually the father for boys.

"My Problem and How I Solved It"

My husband and I wanted to add a patio off the sliding glass door in the back of our house. I wanted to hire someone and get it done quickly; he wanted to save money by installing it himself. He won.

We bought a couple of tons of bricks, which were dumped in the yard.

They sat there for two years.

While the bricks killed the grass, our boys continually tracked mud in the house. Day in and day out, I cleaned up the mud mess. Until I finally lost it. One rainy day, I instructed the boys to stomp around in the mud flat—I mean patio—then dance on the floor next to the door. It was disgusting, but I didn't clean it up.

The mud mess was there when hubby got home from work. He took the hint and started building the patio that weekend.

Roberta T., Santa Clara, California

TRUE STORY

One father must have been awed by toilet training. The first time he saw his son use the potty, the father brought the full bowl to his wife in the kitchen and said, "What am I supposed to do with this?"

Never one to make things too easy, the wife replied, "I usually drink it."

STUPID MEN TRICK

Some people, especially those in the suburbs with ready access to exciting Tupperware parties, store their hams in plastic containers called "ham keepers." Go ahead and pop the ham in the oven without taking it out of this plastic storage container. It adds a whole new taste sensation to "honey-glazed."

Men in labor

According to *Fatherhood in America,* 90 percent of the country's fathers attend their child's birth. Their presence is a source of strength for the mothers. It is also a source of material for stand-up comedians. As men struggle with the strain of participating in the birthing process for the first time in the history of modern society, they do some pretty funny things.

When my first child was born, I had back labor, a particularly visceral type of pain. (I begged for painkillers, but my pleading came either too soon—or too late—in the birthing process.) The nurse asked my husband to apply counterpressure by rubbing my lower back with a tennis ball. As the minutes dragged by, I felt the ball rolling around on my bottom, not my back. When this continued for too long, I looked over my shoulder to see why my husband was so off-base with the massage. I discovered *he was reading the sports section of the newspaper and wasn't watching where he was rubbing!* Could he be any less concerned with my life-producing agony? Oh, how I wished men could give birth!

Debbie Gibson, a mother in Ohio, also had back labor requiring the assistance of a devoted partner. Her nurse recommended applying a warm washcloth. But Gibson's nervous husband was so eager to help that he didn't let the water warm up, and he didn't wring out the washcloth. When he slapped the cloth against her back, it was dripping wet and freezing cold—not very soothing. "Oh yeah, that helped!" Gibson adds.

Connie Williams of Hartford, Connecticut, now laughs about her transportation woes when she had to get to the hospital quickly. Her husband said he'd get her Honda out of the garage while she packed her bag. "We can't take the Honda!" she exclaimed. "It's low on gas and we'll never make it to the hospital!" "Well, we can't take my Volvo station wagon," her husband replied. "The hospital is in a bad neighborhood and I can't risk anything happening to that car! I'll call an ambulance," he said quickly.

They took the Volvo.

When Steve Rupe's first child was born, it was during the Stone Age when men weren't allowed in the delivery room. He dropped off his wife—who was alarmed because she was bleeding—at the emergency entrance and asked the staff not to take her upstairs until he returned from parking the car. They ignored his request, so he ignored their orders to stay downstairs and took the elevator to the third floor. He was met by the security staff, who barred his entrance to the maternity ward. Rupe's wife was not oblivious to the commotion he caused, so she was relieved to receive the note he sent in—"I love you. It's okay to name him Steve."

My mother had labor pains when her daughter-in-law gave birth on the other side of the world, and she vomited the morning I went into labor with my second child. Irvin Feldman of New York was not receiving any telepathic messages when *his* wife went into labor. Feldman was visiting a hospital as an insurance auditor the afternoon his wife's contractions began. He received several messages from his supervisor to stop what he was doing and come to the supervisor's office immediately. Feldman resisted. In fact, he worked through three such messages until the supervisor tracked him down personally to tell him his wife was giving birth in another hospital. Feldman says he made the forty-five-minute drive from Brooklyn to Queens in about fifteen minutes.

Barbara and Kevin Nixon's baby wasn't due for six weeks, so Kevin really enjoyed himself at a friend's wedding reception. They stopped at a supermarket on the way home, even though, as Barbara explains, "He was in no condition to drive even the shopping cart." After they arrived home with the groceries, Barbara's water broke and she knew the baby's arrival was imminent—and quite early. With the help of a pot of coffee and the aerobic exercise that comes with running around an apartment in a state of panic, Kevin sobered up. They made it to the hospital safely and had a son.

When Annie Bliss was giving birth to their second child, her hungry husband left the hospital to get something to eat. The nurse told him he'd have about half an hour. Father Bliss was gone exactly thirty minutes and arrived when Annie couldn't wait any longer to push. Dad walked back in after the doctor had moved into position to play catch.

Steven Henke's story best summarizes perhaps the female perspective on all of this. His child was born four weeks premature and spent time in the neonatal intensive care unit. On the way to one nursery visit Henke stopped into his prenatal class, which he didn't need anymore. The group was hungry for tales from the front, so Henke sat in the front of the class, "like an object on display," and talked about the experiences he and his wife had with the birthing process. "When I told about my wife's contractions, one of the expectant mothers asked, 'Did she take any drugs?' When I answered yes, the women in this class, who were there learning to give birth naturally, all exploded in unison with cheers and applause!"

No story about men in labor would be complete without referring to the classic male line, *"Ooooohhhhh,* I don't think I can do this," when the woman goes into labor. If men gave birth, we'd achieve zero population growth in no time.

"MY PROBLEM AND HOW I SOLVED IT"

No matter where I am in the house, the children always run to me when there's a problem. They can be sitting next to their father on the couch, but as soon as someone gets hurt or has an argument, they come looking for me. (It doesn't help that their father doesn't say, "Wait! I'll take care of that for you!") To teach them how to manage without me, I leave the house to exercise or run errands. That forces the kids and my husband to relate to each other while I get a few minutes to myself.

Joanne V., Fremont, Nebraska

TRUE STORY

The lady of the house called home from work to tell her husband she'd be late and he'd have to fix supper for the kids. She suggested he make Kraft macaroni and cheese. "Geez," he whined, "I hate to cook!" Compare him with another man, who insisted he couldn't make the same meal because he couldn't follow the directions on the box. . . .

STUPID MEN TRICK

If a black sock has a hole in it that shows over the top of your shoe, cover your exposed skin with black Magic Marker.

It's parenting, not babysitting!

Not too long ago, a half-dozen mothers of young children in my conservative suburban neighborhood were scheduling an evening out at a nearby restaurant. The coordinating mom called me and asked, "Can you meet us at my house at seven-thirty? Does that give you enough time to get the kids to bed?" My response was automatic: "Oh, bedtime isn't a problem. Bill will put the girls to bed." Her response surprised me, but in hindsight, I should have expected it. "Well! Aren't *you* lucky!" she exclaimed with surprise. "No," I replied quickly. *"Lucky* is me sleeping with Tommy Lee Jones. *Luck* has nothing to do with my husband putting his children to bed."

On another occasion, a female acquaintance stopped me on the street to say she had seen my husband with our two young daughters buying a newspaper at the supermarket on Sunday morning, and she was *so* impressed. "I think it's just wonderful that he takes both girls with him to get the paper!" she exclaimed. "Yes, he's a swell guy," I mumbled. As I shuffled along, I wondered, "Does she tell my husband how special *I* am after she sees me in the store every week with both daughters and a cartload of groceries costing $80?"*

Women who struggle with their husbands' perception that they're "babysitting," not "parenting," when alone with the children are often battling not only against men's attitudes, but against women's as well. Today's young mothers are as likely as anybody to say to the hapless fellow at the park or at Kmart, "Oh, I see you're babysitting today!"

So who's parenting, and who's babysitting? That depends on your perspective and your expectations. If you want a man to "parent," you need to "raise the expectations at home of what you expect the man to do with the kids," advises Ted Cohen, who studies men and parenting as a sociologist at Ohio Wesleyan University. Unfortunately, some men expect a pat on the back for doing the simplest little things, Cohen adds.

Men are often viewed as "mother's helpers," or as Richard Louv expresses it, "as a second-class mother, not a first-class father. He's seen as an employee of the mother, which can be difficult for him to deal with." Louv, a columnist for *Parents* magazine and author of *Father Love,* says that, oftentimes, women who want

---

*Actually, it's $100 worth but I save $20 with coupons and sales. To learn how men shop, see Chapter 3.

their mates more involved with the children send double messages. "They're not sure they want to share the nurturing role. It is
a powerful role, and as long as women are not secure when moving
to the workplace about their power at work, they're going to be
unlikely to fully share that power in the home," he explains.

Part of the reluctance, Louv concedes, often has to do with a
woman's confidence level in the father. "What fathers say often is
that they find that they can't do things right. They don't do the
laundry, they don't load the dishwasher the way their wives do—
therefore, it's the wrong way. Actually, often it's a different way,"
he explains.

Still, when it comes to confidence level, most women are not
talking about whether the shirt Dad picks out matches the shorts.
It's the safety of the children when left alone with dad that worries
them. "Why is it they get hurt only when they're with their fathers?" a friend asked me recently as we passed a child crying on
the sidewalk. She knows there's hardly a mother in America today
who can't share a story similar to the one I heard recently: A
mother of three children under the age of three left them in the
care of their father at a lake cottage while she ran an errand. She
returned to find all three children hanging off the dock—in the
lake—while Dad was reading the newspaper, oblivious to the potential tragedy looming just yards away.

In a situation like that, it's hard not to be critical. It's incredibly
difficult, in fact, to even be civil. The "Hey, my way is just as good
as your way—it's just different" defense doesn't hold up in matters
of life or death, not even when your lawyer is Robert Shapiro. You
either maintain reasonable standards for safety and keep an eye
on the children constantly—because you *have* to—or you put the
well-being of your children in jeopardy. A man's inability to recognize this scares the bejesus out of his partner because this is one
time when you don't want him to have to learn the hard way.

In spite of this, and in spite of the male willingness to back out
the door to the golf course because of his own admitted incompetence with the children, men are capable of parenting just as well
as women are. And their involvement with their children is just as
important as the mother's. Men have the potential; women need to

take the time to teach them the basics and give them enough lee-way to do it themselves.

"Men use their incompetence, as well as their wife's ambiva-lance about their nurturing role, unfortunately, to their supposed advantage as an excuse for not doing more nurturing and not doing more chores around the house. It reinforces the stereotype of the husband who's all thumbs around the house or around the children," explains Louv with frustration. Cohen agrees. "We make it okay for a man who feels like he's all thumbs to vacate, or to show his discomfort or incompetence," he says. "Somebody will always step in—his mother, or partner—to do it for him."

The other more acceptable excuse some men have for not being as involved as their spouses would like is the subtle discrimination that exists in the workplace. "Highly involved men aren't going to boast about it at work because they aren't going to get any praise or value from their buddies," advises Cohen. More importantly, employers frown on men who take time away from the work rou-tine to attend a school play or chauffeur a child to piano lessons when the carpool system breaks down. When I was out of town on business, my husband-the-executive had to take our young daugh-ter to the pediatrician. His male colleagues were shocked. "Isn't that what you have a wife for?" they asked. Apparently not.

"A woman in the workplace who says her children are a priority is at risk of being treated as a second-class employee. A man who does the same risks not only being a second-class employee but being viewed as a second-class man. Men face extraordinary social pressures, some of them almost unconscious, that shape his fa-thering and encourage his resistance," observes Louv. "In a soci-ety where there is great prejudice against men who are involved with children, it takes a hell-bent personality to break that stereo-type. It often takes two hell-bent personalities—a man and his wife—to break that stereotype."

Cohen also believes men might resist parenting because it is seen as feminine, as something in the woman's area of expertise. Many men, he notes, do not want to be identified with anything feminine. These are men who won't wear a pink shirt or buy a box of tampons at the drugstore, but when it comes to purchasing condoms, are comfortable saying in a loud voice, "Honey, do you think these are big enough?" A man who is paranoid about being mistaken for a woman is a hopeless case. Chances are, he's married to a woman who is reluctant to give up any aspect of the nurturing role anyway. While she might grumble to her friends about her husband's hunting weekends, she actually finds it easier to have him out of the house, which is her domain.

She sings a new tune if their financial picture changes and she has to find a job, though. She is no longer available to do everything, and one area where it's easiest for him to become involved is parenting. Even then, fathers tend to take on the more fun tasks—taking the children to the movies, reading stories aloud, or playing round after round after round of Candyland. This leaves Mom more time to soak in the tub, head to the mall, read a novel—ha, ha, just kidding—do laundry, mop the floor, and change sheets.

"Men and women do parent differently," Cohen comments. "Men tend to do more of the play than the work."

Experts say that more men are becoming more involved as parents for several reasons—some don't want to repeat the mistakes of their own absentee fathers, others are disillusioned by their jobs and are seeking other ways to build their identities, some are forced into it because of the time constraints of two-income households, while others truly believe that sharing the responsibility equally is right, natural, and fair. The increasing numbers of fathers at parent-teacher nights or at soccer practice indicate a better attitude on the part of men . . . or a lack of choices.

But these men still are not representative of the entire population. There are more uninvolved fathers or marginally involved fathers than there are fully involved fathers—the men who truly share at least 50 percent of the parenting struggles and pleasures. And the problems caused by missing fathers are a separate story—and not a happy one.

The key to happiness in this area must have something to do with really, really knowing your partner before you start a family. What kind of a man is he? A workaholic is not going to change as soon as a newborn arrives home. Typically, a new father's work hours increase to compensate for the new mother's decrease in income. (That's one theory. The other one is that he can't stand the crying so he avoids being home.) Is he a macho man—can you picture him changing messy diapers, or will that be too feminine? Or is he a Sensitive New Age Guy, one who derives part of his identity from being more forward-thinking than his father or brothers? He will probably be as involved as possible—and if you want him to be involved, you must *let* him be involved.

It is just as important to know yourself. Are you capable of giving up some of your power to your baby's father? Are you willing to let him learn how to identify diarrhea or to take a sick infant to the doctor's office—without you there to interpret or take notes? When he brings home a high-tech skin-sensitive thermometer instead of the traditional "insert in rectum here" device your mother always used, can you bite your tongue and acknowledge that using the rectal method really is a pain in the butt, so to speak anyway?

Parenting is one of the most difficult jobs anybody will ever have, but it is also one of the most rewarding. It would be a shame to exclude any father from the frustrations and joys of the challenge, even if he's one whose idea of serving dinner to the gang is to order a pizza and plop everyone in front of the television set.

Hey. It could be worse. He could be teaching preschoolers how to row a boat—when he's not in the boat. Or letting a toddler play with a chainsaw in the house, while he's in another room watching a football game. ("Well, gee, the chainsaw wasn't turned on. Besides, I can patch up those scratches in the wood floor.") Or letting the first-grader go-cart down the middle of the street at dusk. *Hmmm. . . .* I'd take back my position that men are just as competent as women, but I have an appointment with my masseuse. Then I'm spending twenty minutes in the sauna. After that, I'm meeting some friends for a movie. That's if I'm *lucky* and my husband will put the kids to bed.

DAD DETAILS

How involved are fathers with their children? Here are the facts:

- Fathers spend about three hours a week on primary child-care (feeding, dressing, bathing), compared to nine hours by mothers.
- More than half the time fathers spend with their children is interactional—considered the most enjoyable and influential time parents spend with their children.
- Men aged thirty-five to sixty-four still spend less time with their children than the mothers do, but the gap is smaller than with other age groups.
- Only 30 percent of all married fathers with a preschooler say they do three or more hours of childcare chores a day.
- Most fathers whose oldest child is school-aged say they read to the child or help with homework at least once a week.
- Nearly five times as many men would rather be viewed by their families as sensitive and caring than as rugged and masculine.
- Three-fourths of all fathers don't regularly take any responsibility for the daily care of their children.
- Father-child interplay (the fun stuff) among children from kindergarten to tenth grade averages a half hour to two and a half hours per day.
- More than 60 percent of involved fathers are actually just "mother's helper."

DADS PARENT DIFFERENTLY

A debate among those who have time for such matters—mostly men—surrounds the value of parenting styles. Should the father be a "mother's helper" or should he follow his instincts and rough-house with the kids? Should he be more nurturing? Children don't need two mothers, some say. They need a mother *and* a father. Key ways men parent differently from Jerrold Lee Shapiro, Ph.D., author of *The Measure of a Man* include:

- Fathers use physical contact to excite a child; mothers use it to comfort and provide security. Dad tickles or wrestles; Mom hugs.
- When playing, fathers direct the activity, acting as a teacher with the child as an apprentice. Mothers play at the child's level, side-by-side, allowing the child to be in charge and run the show. Father's play also encourages children to experiment, learn new skills, and push against their limits.
- Fathers discipline with inflexible rules; mothers discipline according to the moment, adjusting to the child's mood.
- Fathers communicate by teaching. Conversations between fathers and children are short and occur side-by-side rather than face-to-face. Mothers communicate more emotionally, sharing feelings and enjoying long conversations.
- A mother's love is unconditional; a father's is tied to performance.
- Mothers worry about a newborn's survival, fathers about the child's future success.

TIPS ON HOW TO PARENT "50-50"

50-50 Parenting author Gayle Kimball, Ph.D., and others offer these tips for fathers who want to be more involved in the parenting of their children:

- Spend equal time with your baby beginning at birth. Feed it in the middle of the night, change diapers, go to the pediatrician's for checkups.
- Schedule regular time alone with your children.
- Remind your wife that she should not impose her standards on you when you are with the children.

- Don't rely on your wife for your information about parenting. Read books and articles; talk to others about their experiences.
- Reduce television viewing, substituting for that conversations with your child. Put your children to bed; drive them to activities.
- Plan regular weekly fun activities.
- Make a conscious effort to stop assigning the "fun" or "easy" tasks for yourself. One way to help minimize housework and parenting inequities is to develop a chores chart that divides weekly responsibilities, both social and administrative. Rotate tasks so everybody has an opportunity to do both the fun and the not-so-fun chores. This helps eliminate the nonproductive "men's work" and "women's work" attitudes.
- Evaluate the amount of time invested in work and other nonparenting activities to determine if it interferes with your ability to be a 50-50 father. Make changes if necessary.
- Talk with your father about his hindsight on parenting.
- Press for social supports for involved fathers, including parental leave and flexible work hours. Become a role model for others too chicken to stand out in the workplace.

"MY PROBLEM AND HOW I SOLVED IT"

Ever since my oldest daughter was able to crawl, I've worried about her safety. Actually, I was worried about that before she was born—was the umbilical cord wrapped around her neck? What if she slipped out of the doctor's hands during the delivery?

When she learned to stand, I worried she would fall into the toilet and drown, or pull her father's razor off the sink and slit her lovely little wrists, or tumble down the stairs and break her neck, become paralyzed for life, and blame me, the only person who ever tried to protect her.

My husband never worried. He'd leave the toilet seat up, the hairdryer plugged in next to the sink, the medicine on the counter. It drove me crazy.

My solution? Every time he broke an essential safety guideline, I tossed a *Sports Illustrated* in the diaper pail. He's never fished one out, and the children now have a safer home.

Mary G., Petersburg, Virginia

TRUE STORY

Do men think women have an extra gene that makes them more immune to the smell of a dirty diaper? One woman tells her story:

"When my son was a baby, my husband took care of him when I had to run errands. For some reason, I often returned to find a few clean cloth diapers wadded up on the diaper pail. Turns out Dad was tying them around his face as an odor mask while changing messes! He bagged the mask for Child No. 2 because we switched to disposables, and it would have hurt too much to pull the tapes off his face . . . or out of his hair."

STUPID MEN TRICK

Don't bother with the complicated instructions that come with those one-piece rompers for your baby. Put the arms through the legs, the legs through the arms, and snap up the back, not the front. The kid will never notice.

⁕ *8* ⁕

Beyond the
ᴠ Stone Tablet ᴠ

∽∾

As women evolved, they acquired communication skills. As far as researchers can tell, this did not happen with men. Women complain that men don't listen, don't talk, don't respond. Men respond by saying, "I'll listen when you say something worth hearing." In truth, men *do* communicate—they just do it differently.

Male Answering Syndrome:
The cause, the cure

Male Answering Syndrome (MAS) is a recently identified disorder referring to the male tendency to provide an answer to (1) a question *other than* the one asked, (2) a question *before* it is asked, and (3) a question before it is asked *completely*. Men, you see, have many, many answers, and are eager to present them. For men afflicted with MAS, the answers are one size fits all.

Underneath this horrible, horrible affliction is the male need to share what he knows. The need to share facts. The need to participate in communication one-upsmanship. It's as if the guy is saying, "I'm so much smarter than you that I can answer your question before you're even sure what your question is!" As a result, behavior that is intended to show off a male superiority we might otherwise overlook is often misinterpreted as rude. In other words, when your brother answers questions directed at you instead of allowing you to speak for yourself, he is not suggesting you are too stupid to know the answer. He is more likely attempting to prove that he is the smartest person in the room—but he does this at your expense.

Sigh.

Boys, boys, boys! When will you ever learn that it's the *women* you need to impress, not the other *men!* And women are rarely impressed by men who dominate all conversation. They are more likely to be bowled over by a guy who offers an appropriate gift on the actual day of the occasion, not two weeks later.

Marvin Wray, co-author of *First Class Male* and ministerial director of the Potomac Conference, says MAS represents a man's need to let everyone know he's in control. "If you're in charge, you're the one who answers the questions," he observes. Wray's wife has accused him of dominating conversations as well, but he's quick to remind her that, as a minister, he's paid to talk. "Yes, but you're not paid by the word," she reminds him before she answers the question herself.

"He never wants to admit there is an area he knows nothing about because that would mean admitting weakness and vulnerability. It's just kind of built into us that we're not supposed to admit that we don't know something," adds Robert Pasick, Ph.D., a Michigan psychologist and author of *What Every Man Needs to Know*. (Tip #42 in his book: "Generally, asking good questions is more productive than trying to come up with all the right answers.")

Pasick sees MAS as yet another way that men try to fix things. A question indicates a problem; an answer is the solution that fixes the problem. "A man measures his self-worth on how well and how effective he is as a fixer," he explains. "There's no area out of his expertise."

Jim Hasenhauer, a speech communications professor at the University of California at Northridge, observes, "It's part of a broader behavioral response which is that males are instrumental—they are always trying to accomplish or do things. That's how they measure themselves," he explains. "When a male hears a question, he hears a request for information, help, or assistance or some kind of an indication that the other person doesn't know the answer," Hasenhauer observes.

Even if nobody's asking *him* the question?

Especially if he's not asked the question.

"This gives him an opportunity to show what he knows. He's using language to insert himself in a situation," Hasenhauer explains. (Translation: The guy is butting in.) It's just another way that men use language to compete and show their status in a group, an adult version of "mine's bigger than yours."

Hasenhauer says that, in a man's world, there are two kinds of questions. A question is either a test, where the asker knows the answer and is seeing if the other person can answer it, or it's a direct request for information. With women, a question is often a way to keep a conversation going. Women also use questions to distract the man afflicted with MAS so he doesn't notice something you'd like to hide from him—your lover sneaking out the bathroom window, for example.

The male game playing is something we can walk around or avoid in most cases. MAS becomes an issue, though, in the workplace when a woman is deprived of the opportunity to show what she knows by a dominating dimwit whose life is so empty that his biggest thrill is hearing his own voice. Most women will not try to play verbal chicken, outshouting the man who insists on answering questions asked of someone else. It should not, however, be beneath any woman to say in a straightforward and calm manner, "Thank you for your insight, but Tom asked *me* the question. My answer is . . ."

In personal situations, such as a party or other social gathering, Pasick suggests clarifying with your male companion your definition of what you find attractive in a man. "Tell him you think he's especially sexy when he's listening, not talking," Pasick advises. Wray would like to see more women speak up with confidence, saying, "I'm perfectly capable of answering my own questions." He adds that, if that doesn't work, an elbow in the ribs probably would help. It might also help to offer positive reinforcement—a hug or a special toy—on the rare occasions when your male companion *does* let you answer a question.

Pasick fears that men just do not value a woman's voice. "It's a kind of general thing—a woman's opinion isn't considered that important." It is important to be aware of this bias and to address it strategically. For example, don't even bother to *try* to answer questions in a conversation about sports, even if you're one of the three women on the planet who actually know more about sports than men. Make your contribution to questions related to children, cooking, or the home—traditional female domains.

Once you have established your authority in these areas—which will take time, by the way—you can move on to more nontraditional areas where you have expertise that has been overlooked so far. Eventually, you'll be answering questions about politics—or even answering questions nobody asked you! Before you know it, you'll tell people about the problems in corporate America without anyone even inquiring about them! Soon, you'll be lecturing at cocktail parties on how CD-ROM works, or how to get rid of moles in your yard. Why, you might even answer a question about tuck-pointing! That is, if anyone still invites you to anything. Remember, nobody likes a know-it-all. Well, nobody except another guy. And that's only because it presents an opportunity to show he knows even *more*.

"My Problem and How I Solved It"

My children grew tired of the way their father hogged the TV remote control. Before he came home from work one night, the kids removed the batteries. Because Dad had to get out of the chair to change the channel, he did it less often and the kids could actually watch an entire thirty-minute program.

Barbara M., Sarasota, Florida

True Story

A survey from a tire manufacturer tells us that 38 percent of the fellows questioned said they love their cars more than their women. Perhaps those men should be traded in for better models. . . .

Stupid Men Trick

Your wife is away at the beach with the kids while you're left behind to slave away, earning a paycheck. The last thing you need to worry about is clean sheets. Sleep on one side of the bed the first week, then switch sides for the second week.

"Well, why didn't you ask?"

If *Jeopardy* had a show just for men, the topics across the board would be Sports, Beer, Chicks, Locker Room Smells, Cars, Rude Noises, Expensive Electronics, Take Out or Delivery?, and Gadgets.

"I'll take Expensive Electronics for twenty dollars, Alex," booms Jack. "Okay, Jack, the answer is 'six percent,' " responds host Trebek. Jack rings in with the answer. "The percentage of female subscribers of *Stereo Review!*" he shouts. "Use the correct form for the answer," Trebek reminds him yet again, impatiently. "Uh, what is the percentage of female subscribers of *Stereo Review?*" Jack responds, not the least bit embarrassed.

Men aren't big on questions. And when they *do* concede to ask one or two, the questions are usually limited to topics they're interested in. They are particularly nonquizzical when it comes to social subjects, as illustrated by this actual conversation overheard recently:

The telephone rings at the home of Beth and John. John answers it. They are being invited to dinner. When Beth returns to the room, she asks John a few questions:

Beth: "Who was that?" *John:* "Mark Murphy."
Beth: "What did he want?" *John:* "He invited us to dinner next weekend."
Beth: "Saturday or Sunday?" *John:* "I don't know."
Beth: "What time?" *John:* "I don't know."
Beth: "Are the kids invited?" *John:* "I don't know."
Beth: "Should we bring anything?" *John:* "I don't know."

Beth: "Is anyone else invited?" *John:* "I don't know."

Beth: "Why didn't you ask more questions?" *John:* "I don't know."

Beth needs more information, but not because she is writing the neighborhood newsletter. She needs to know if she should call a babysitter, whether she should shop for food to bring, or even what is appropriate apparel for the situation. A casual potluck supper with another family is not the same as a sit-down candlelit dinner for eight. But John, apparently, just doesn't get it.

Neither do other guys, according to Dayle Hardy-Short, assistant professor of communication at Idaho State University. "There's a significant body of research that suggests that, in general, men ask significantly fewer questions than women do," she reports. With regards to married couples, studies show that women ask 85 to 90 percent of the questions, she says, noting that one study puts that number as high as 96 percent.

Bob Garfield, a commentator for National Public Radio and an advertising critic for *Advertising Age* magazine, is a professional question asker. He reassures us that, "It's not that men don't understand enough to ask the questions—it simply reflects the sheer joy we get from being sullen and uncommunicative." In addition, Garfield believes women are seeking answers to questions on subjects men don't care about.

"If I'm speaking to a friend whose wife just had a baby, I'll probably go through all the boilerplate questions. But unless the weight is volunteered to me, I won't ask about it. Unless they have specific requests for a gift, I won't make inquiries about what they need. And whether I remember the answers to these questions by the time I get debriefed by my wife is another matter altogether," Garfield explains.

Garfield's observations highlight a key difference in how men and women communicate, reports Norman Goldner, Ph.D., a professor at University of Detroit Mercy and co-author of *Why Women and Men Don't Get Along.* "The point of communication for men is often to solve a problem but, for women, it's a social exchange," he notes. Sometimes a woman's interest in information stems more from her social relationship than it does from her actual need to know.

"Men aren't quite so programmed to ask questions," observes Helane Levine-Keating, Ph.D., professor of English at Pace University in New York City. "When I'm talking to male friends, I notice there are certain things they neglect to ask. They don't want a lot of details about an experience." But women feel more in control of their world with that kind of detailed information, Levine-Keating says.

"Men often find these kinds of questions to be time wasters," agrees Hardy-Short in Idaho. "Researchers speculate that the function of question-asking is to keep the conversation going. Questions are used to indicate support, to avoid imposing one's opinion on others, and to accommodate other people's feelings or opinions." Not exactly your typical male description, because men aren't socialized to be polite or to worry about other people's opinions.

Hardy-Short also notes that men are often uncomfortable asking questions women wouldn't hesitate to blurt out. Men view some kinds of questions as prying, and are more likely to wait for the information to be volunteered. Which means that when your husband's best friend calls and says his wife left him, it might be unrealistic to expect your husband to ask his friend the obvious— "Why?"—even though it's the first question you would ask. (This also means you shouldn't grab the phone from your husband and demand "Why?" yourself. The male friend won't want to tell you any more than he wants to tell your husband.)

Garfield believes men don't ask more questions because they are genetically incapable of doing so. "It's my theory that men do not ask questions and therefore are unable to provide answers when their wives want them because the same chromosome in women has an altogether different effect. In women, the chromosome that keeps men uninquisitive causes women to carefully open gifts so as not to damage the wrapping paper."

Then, of course, there's the issue of "domain," Levine-Keating points out. The social life is in the woman's domain whereas the "exterior world" is considered the man's turf. "Women are trained to handle the social calendar and men aren't, so it doesn't occur to them to ask the right questions for the information we need regarding personal matters."

Even so, the inability to ask questions spills over to the workplace as well, Hardy-Short, observes. "Despite the number of questions women ask at home or at work, the man determines the topic of conversation. Studies show women introduce the topic just 36 percent of the time," she says. "In fact, men do more talking, they talk longer, they talk more when interrupted, and they interrupt more often." There. She got that out before she was interrupted.

Commentator Garfield believes it's fruitless for women to expect any other kind of behavior from their men. "I think women's energies would be much better devoted to channeling man's energies into something else that may be useful. There's something culturally and behaviorally imprinted on us that makes it a waste of women's psychic energy to get men to be more inquisitive and valuable. He's just not going to ask a lot of questions about things he's not interested in."

This philosophy can actually be liberating when adopted by women. Do you really care about the details for next Sunday's golf date, or the fact that Pete's car broke down and he needs a ride to work, or how the deadline on the big project at the office got moved up? Then don't trouble your pretty little head with such trivia when the phone rings. That way, when your male companion asks about the phone messages—*if* you bothered to take any—just say, "I don't know." It might feel *really* good.

"MY PROBLEM AND HOW I SOLVED IT"

Our office has a communal coffeepot that goes dry quickly. Unfortunately, the men aren't too willing to make a new pot. They'll let an empty pot smoke on the burner before they'll open a new coffee pouch.

The women in the group got together and agreed to limit how often they'd refill the coffeemaker. We decided that, for every time we made a new pot, we wouldn't make a new pot the next time.

For a long time, we'd hear the guys saying things like, "Hey, who used up the coffee?" or "How come there's no coffee?" or "There's no coffee!" We acted as if we didn't hear it. After a few weeks, most of them miraculously learned how to make a pot of coffee. Those who didn't still have headaches from the caffeine withdrawal.

Marcia L., Detroit, Michigan

TRUE STORY

How do you get a man's attention when you're competing with 132 channels on the television and the newspaper sports section?

When it's really, really important and he isn't responding, place a stack of catalogs next to the telephone. Then pick up the receiver, wave a credit card under his nose, and sing, "I'm dialing!"

Works like a charm.

STUPID MEN TRICK

It's Tuesday night. You're bored. Bake pork chops in the oven by placing them directly on the rack, without a drip pan. Watch the flames flare as the grease hits the heating element.

Male support groups: The solution to women's problems?

A couple of Californians—who else?—are promoting a concept called "gender reconciliation" as a solution to the problems women are having with men. Their technique requires men to acknowledge that a problem exists and then—get this—*meet with a group of other men who can admit they have problems.*

Therapist Aaron Kipnis, Ph.D., believes bringing the sexes together to discuss problems is particularly useful when women complain that men don't do "their share" of work around the house. Kipnis, a man, says women often overlook or forget certain more manly chores handled by those maligned fellows. "How many women climb a ladder to clean gutters? How many women change the oil in the car? Or get on the roof to fix the TV antenna?" Kipnis queries. And how many men work full-time, grocery shop, do laundry, change loaded diapers, prepare meals, *and* provide family transportation on a daily basis?

While it probably helps women to be reminded of the accomplishments of men, the guys still can't prove—even in these groups—that they carry 50 percent of the load at home. So, Kipnis says, they bring in other issues, such as how they die younger, have a higher suicide rate, and so on.

Stretching? You bet.

Kipnis, Ph.D., and Elizabeth Hingston of the Pangaea Institute for Gender Studies in Santa Barbara, California, travel across the country conducting workshops designed to help men and women duke it out on neutral ground. They encourage men and women to meet first in single-sex support groups to vent, then meet together in combined sex groups to share with the opposite sex their frustrations, disappointment, anger, or in the case of men, bewilderment.

The concept of women meeting to discuss problems has been around since the days of the caveman. Many participate in informal man-bashing sessions anyway—often with men in the next room. But getting men together in support groups is a task. As Kipnis notes, groups of men will talk about sports or job issues before they'll share feelings about relationships.

Worse yet, Kipnis says the man has to acknowledge there's a problem before he'll attend a support group meeting. "The man has to be desirous of improving his relationships," Kipnis confesses.

When men do join groups, Kipnis says, it's because "they feel alienated, isolated, and alone. Men have a longing for friendship and community that is not satisfied by superficial relationships with football buddies."

Communicating with other men in a structured setting supposedly helps these guys establish better relationships while it helps them define and articulate what bothers *them* about women. According to Kipnis, a common complaint is that women don't say what they mean.

"Men tell us they rarely hear women say, 'This is what I want, like, don't want, or don't like.' As a result, they don't know when they've offended women," Kipnis says.

This is especially important in the workplace, where people

have become paranoid—and confused—about sexual harassment. How can they know what's appropriate, men tell Kipnis in group sessions, when women don't come right out and tell them they don't like what's just been said or done?

"What is perfectly acceptable in male culture is not acceptable in female culture, and men aren't familiar with female culture," Kipnis notes. "In male territory, when you step too closely into another man's space, one man will give the other a signal. But men don't experience those boundary signals with women."

Or maybe they just don't hear or see them.

Are the revelations in these group sessions helpful? Some women are reassured to know their problems aren't unique. Others are discouraged to hear, "See? They're all alike," or "He can't help it, it's genetic."

All too often this "genetic issue" becomes the male excuse for walking around the juice puddle on the floor or letting the trash overflow. "Hey, I'm just a man. I don't notice these things," they say.

The bigger question is whether the support groups promoted by Kipnis and his colleague will help us spend less time whining about men. They might, but the situation brings to mind the old joke about how many psychologists it takes to change a light-bulb. The answer is, "One, but the lightbulb really has to want to change." If the men involved don't want to change, this probably won't work.

"MY PROBLEM AND HOW I SOLVED IT"

When my husband places his clothes on hangers, he doesn't do it very carefully, and the clothes, especially slacks, get very wrinkled or creased in the wrong places. Then, when he puts them on, he says, "Is this too messy to wear?" I tell him, "Yes," but I no longer jump for the iron. Instead, I show him how to hang them up properly—again—and suggest he wear something else. I think if I do this for another year, he'll catch on.

Catherine H., Wauwautosa, Wisconsin

TRUE STORY

She collapsed in a chair after a long Sunday combining office work with laundry, child care, meal preparation and minor household repairs. "Why," she asked her mate, "are you comfortable letting me do so much—even the repairs?"

He smiled. "Because you don't know how to motivate me," he replied.

STUPID MEN TRICK

Don't bother with the laundry. Take as many items as you can to the dry cleaner—but not your underwear. That's too embarrassing. Toss that in a pile on the floor. When the pile smells too foul (as opposed to kind of foul), throw everything out and buy new skivvies.

"What did you mean by that?"

Ann and Tom are celebrating their anniversary at an expensive restaurant. She dresses up for the occasion, wearing a new outfit her husband hasn't seen. Waltzing into the living room, Ann twirls around and says, "Well, what do you think?"

Tom glances up briefly and says, "You look great," before turning back to the sports report on TV.

"Do you like this dress?" Ann asks.

"Sure," Tom says over his shoulder. "It's nice."

"Do you like it better than my blue dress?" she persists.

"Yes, I suppose I do," he answers.

"What's wrong with my blue dress?" Ann asks with an edge in her voice. "Does it make me look fat?"

"*Hmm?* Oh—no—it doesn't make you look fat," he replies, confused.

"Well, then why do you like this one more? I thought you liked my blue dress!" she pouts.

Tom turns off the TV and grabs his car keys. "Let's go," he says as he puts his hand on Ann's elbow to steer her to the door. "We'll be late."

As the car backs out of the driveway, Tom wonders what they were just talking about, while Ann stews about the jelly doughnut she wished she hadn't enjoyed with her morning coffee.

It's a typical scenario in male-female communication. Ann asks a question; Tom answers as best as he can with a straightforward, honest response. Ann doesn't accept his statements as direct communication—she wonders if she should read between the lines. Should she?

Laurie Schloff, co-author of *He and She Talk* and a communications consultant at the Speech Improvement Company in Boston, suggests that Ann's interpretation might have to do with how the message is given. "Professional speakers use a skill called vocal variety, which helps them sound interesting. Some people don't have much vocal variety, which can confuse the listener. In this case, the way Tom says, 'That dress is nice,' might not be the way you and I would say that to a friend, so the wife misinterprets her husband's comments because she's misled by his intonation or pattern or vocal variety," Schloff explains.

Schloff also says women sometimes react negatively to the word "*nice.*" "I have a friend who goes bonkers if her husband says she looks nice. She doesn't want to hear 'nice.' She wants a more specific description of how she looks—nice isn't enough." For Schloff's friend, "nice" is a copout. She believes her husband is capable of saying the kinds of things her female friends might say—"Those colors are perfect for you," or "That fabric drapes beautifully on you." Schloff's friend should move to another planet. Unless they're interior decorators, Earthmen do not discuss the cut, color, or flow of women's clothing.

According to Linda Carli, Ph.D., an associate professor of psychology at Wellesley College, men claim to be more direct communicators; women claim to be more indirect. Carli cites studies on gender communication differences based on what people report about their own behavior. "Men claim to use direct means of communication and influence," Carli reports. "They demand; they don't beat around the bush." As in, "Don't ever serve fried squash blossoms again!" or "Tell me right now who put photos of naked men in my locker at the club!"

Linguist Deborah Tannen, Ph.D., reports in her book *Talking from 9 to 5* that men and women are *both* indirect, but that differences in background as well as situations affect their style of communication. In some cases, she reports, direct communication indicates the person's power. In others, the reverse is also true.

Carli says that women tend to be more indirect communicators because they have lower status. In addition, women have been socialized to believe that straightforward communication can be offensive. They don't want to offend, so they avoid a direct approach. They have been taught to be more concerned about the needs of others, so they avoid offending with a direct style. "It's what we might call more polite talk, and to be more polite is to be more indirect," adds Schloff.

Carli studies what men and women actually do, versus what they *say* they do. Observing men and women making a request of strangers and friends, Carli learned:

- Women added a preface to the request.
- Men rarely said please.
- Men got to the point quicker.
- Men used more guilt ploys.
- Women didn't use guilt and were instead very polite, deferential, and kind.

Carli concluded that, especially when communicating to other men, men are more direct, are less polite, and use more guilt. "We associate guilt with mothers, though," she footnotes.

Lou Hampton, a communications and media consultant in Washington D.C. who leads workshops on gender communications differences, suggests whether the man communicates directly, and means what he says, often depends on the subject. "By and large, most men are fairly bottom-line-oriented and tend to say what they want." The exception, he notes, is when it's time to talk about the *f* word: feelings. Even then, it's not that the men are trying to hide or disguise their feelings—it's more likely that they just won't say anything. "They're more guarded about expressing feelings because they fear that, by doing so, they will lose a certain amount of control," Hampton observes.

Generally, experts believe that men communicate more directly than women give them credit for. But that doesn't mean you should take everything at face value. Consider the experience of Mary Harvey of East Lansing, Michigan, who has finally cracked the code her husband uses when commenting on her wardrobe. Here's how it works:

He says:	"Wow, you really look great. Is that new?"
He means:	"I noticed you have a new outfit and I like it."
He says:	"Is that a new outfit?"
He means:	"I noticed you have something new—I don't particularly care for it."
He says:	(Nothing, just gives outfit a once-over.)
He means:	"I noticed you have something new. It totally repulses me but I'm too smart to say so and I hope to God you don't ask me what I think." (If pressed, he will say, "You have other things I like better.")

Notice he didn't tell a single lie.

HE SAID, SHE HEARD

Entire books have been written about how men and women communicate differently. Many times, women read too much into the things men say. Here are a few typical examples of what a man might say, and how a woman interprets it:

He Said	*She Heard*
"Would you like to go out to dinner Saturday night?"	"I hate your cooking!"
"I'm going to Bob's to watch the football game Sunday afternoon."	"You're boring!"
"What's for supper?"	"I haven't read those studies that say men are helping out more at home."
"Do you know where my brown belt is?"	"I married my mother."
"Where's the coffeepot in this office?"	"You are a woman. Serve me."
"I don't feel well."	"Mommy, I'll feel better if you take care of me."
"Did you do something to your hair?"	"You look awful."
"How does this copier work?"	"If I act dumb, you'll do the whole copying job for me. It's easier than showing me how to do it myself."
"Do you usually sort the laundry?"	"I'm going to wash your delicate undies with my new black sweats so you'll never ask me to do laundry again."
"I'm going to the store. Do you need anything?"	"I'm too lazy to look in the cupboards to see what we need. Just tell me what to buy."

"MY PROBLEM AND HOW I SOLVED IT"

My parents live in another state. When I call home, each of them often gets on a different phone extension so I can speak to them both at once. However, when my mother and I want to enjoy "girl talk"—without my dad—we start talking about fabrics and sewing, and he hangs up his phone quickly.

Tiffany G., Bettendorf, Iowa

TRUE STORY

Talk about killing two birds with one stone. When one fellow needed clean jeans *and* a shower, he put the jeans on the floor of the shower stall, poured detergent over them, and stomped on them while he took his shower. By the next day, they were dry and ready for another day on the job.

STUPID MEN TRICK

The casual diner knows the best way to enjoy whipped cream on pie or ice cream is bite by bite. Take a bite of the pie, squirt the whipped cream in your mouth. Another bite, another squirt. Yum!

The passive-aggressive male and you

Thanks to psychologist Scott Wetzler, Ph.D., women can now attach a label to the most frustrating of male behaviors. What used to be referred to as, "I have absolutely no idea why he said something so mean to me in front of my mother," has now been translated to, "My boyfriend is so passive-aggressive!" The good news is, we now know what to call it. The bad news is, we're stuck with it.

In his book *Living with the Passive-Aggressive Man,* Wetzler describes the passive-aggressive man as someone who thinks of himself as weak and powerless, and sees passive-aggression as his only response to people he views as more powerful—his wife, his boss, his mother. Instead of dealing with his problems directly, head-on, he lashes out in subtler and more destructive ways. A passive-aggressive man, Wetzler says, is one who says he forgot to pick up milk on the way home rather than tell you he doesn't want to be bothered with the task. Or starts a project in the house but never finishes it, although he promises regularly that he'll "get right to it."

"Passive-aggression is about what's not done, more than what is done. It's the expression of hostility in relationships but it's done in such an indirect way that it can be denied," Wetzler explains. It leaves the other person scratching her head.

"I know one woman who confronted her boyfriend about why he was never available for a Saturday night date. He had the audacity to say she was too clinging. So instead of talking about his misbehavior, which is what they should have been talking about, he had managed to change the subject to her dependency and neediness and she ended up believing that she was the one with the problem," Wetzler says. "These guys are pretty slippery characters," he adds.

Passive-aggressive behavior, Wetzler says, is marked by obstructionism, chaos, feeling victimized, making excuses and lying, procrastination, chronic lateness and forgetfulness, ambiguity, sulking, and a fear of dependency, intimacy, and competition. (If your companion shows all of these signs, slit your wrists now.) In short, a passive-aggressive man is a real pain in the butt. He turns your world upside down—then blames you. When you dare to complain, he accuses you of being a nagging shrew. He promises, promises, promises, but never delivers. Remarkably, *you have nothing to do with it!*

Daphne Rose Kingma, Ph.D., and author of *The Men We Never Knew*, knows more about men than men do. Her experience counseling individuals and couples has taught her that passive-aggressive behavior comes from the man's unidentified pain and fear, often from the distant past. "Sometimes he has a very deep experience of abandonment that he can't put into words," she explains. He deals with these emotions by indirectly administering pain to someone else—you. "He is the man whose wealthy parents lost their fortune when he was young. He became angry that he had to become a provider rather than continue as a spoiled child.

As an adult, this manifested itself when his wife became the least bit extravagant—he refused to turn off lights so he could waste electricity," explains Kingma, citing an actual case. (Imagine the relief that guy felt when he discovered why he couldn't turn off the lights—not because he was afraid of the dark, but because he was passive-aggressive!)

Verne Becker, author of *The Real Man Inside,* sees other issues at play, as well. "One aspect is the location or domain of the behavior," he begins. "The passive-aggressive man can go to work and be the go-getter and the power-luncher, then come home with the attitude that 'I did all that at work and now that I'm home I want to sit back and be taken care of and not have to bother with the house or diapers or anything else,' " Becker explains. Imagine how well that plays in a two-income household where the woman has also carried her share of the financial load during the day, but comes home to face not a comfy chair and a dry martini but three hungry children with runny noses, a sinkful of dishes, and an answering machine full of messages. Think she'll collapse into the chair with a "Bring me my slippers, I've done my job" attitude? Not a chance. Women display their passive-aggressive nature more tactfully, whereas men are more clumsy and obvious, Wetzler reports.

When you're involved with a passive-aggressive man, it's often difficult to step back and evaluate the situation objectively. The key, Wetzler says, is to watch for the pattern. "What you find with these passive-aggressive people is that they do it persistently, so that a pattern gets set up. That's when you know the excuse is invalid. It really is a problem with an underlying meaning to it, which is that he's not going to give you what you want. That's the whole point—to not satisfy you," he explains. What is perhaps most frightening about this obnoxious behavior is that it is unconscious.

Your own participation can be unconscious as well. Wexler says women involved with passive-aggressive men—which is most men, by the way—are either what he calls "managers," who are too controlling; "rescuers," who treat him like a baby; or "victims," who let themselves be taken advantage of. Recognizing your role is one way to turn the situation around.

Psychologist Kingma, suggests giving your passive-aggressive partner a taste of his own medicine. "Do some passive-aggressive things back to him until he figures it out—let him experience these feelings rather than being told." For example, if your companion consistently calls ahead and says he's on his way and will pick you up in fifteen minutes—but shows up an hour and a half later—turn the tables. Don't be there when he finally does show up. Allow a reasonable grace period for traffic delays—thirty minutes—but disappear after that so you're not waiting for him at the door with your tail wagging like an eager puppy. This also will keep you from growling like an angry dog.

"What happens is the woman ends up frequently doubting herself in some way. She feels guilty, like she's asking too much, or she responds angrily and the fellow says, 'See, you're getting all worked up, you really are an angry witch!' " Wexler says. Don't give him that satisfaction. Get some distance.

Wexler's advice is to keep a clear head. "Stay calm and don't let things escalate. Be realistic about your expectations, and don't make wild generalizations." Then confront him. Kingma recommends being very direct, insisting that he get therapy because the behavior is related to some deep unresolved issues.

"Passive-aggressive behavior is always camouflaging a need or unexpressed feeling—I'm scared, I'm in pain, or I need your attention," Kingma comments. "But most of us are in the dark about our emotional issues."

Becker reminds us that we are fairly powerless in this frustrating drama. "Women have to be able to tell themselves, 'There's nothing I can do to change him or stop him. I'm powerless.' But then remind yourself, 'I am not powerless over myself.' " It is important to be supportive, but not get sucked in. "Say, 'I'm powerless to help you, but I really want you to find help or relief,' and get help for yourself if you need it," Becker adds. "Caring for yourself is your only hope for changing the other person."

Easier said than done, of course. Wexler knows that many

women lack the self-esteem needed for the head-on confrontation required. "These guys throw tremendous smoke in your eyes and you end up losing focus," he warns. Yet without that direct confrontation, where you explain what's unacceptable about the behavior and what you expect in the future, your relationship is just a shell, Kingma cautions. "A relationship can exist as a functional unit, but to have a real, intimate relationship, couples do need therapy," she observes.

Kingma has learned, too, that men who initially get "dragged to the process kicking and screaming" often actually enjoy therapy. "Once men have an opportunity to connect, they don't resist and are very excited about the process," she notes. We must remember, however, that Kingma practices in California, where attitudes are not the same as those in other parts of the country.

Wherever you live, you have a right to live free of the tension generated by this strange behavior. Take Kingma's advice and use the "eye for an eye" approach. When he forgets to bring home milk, forget to buy his beer. When he buys himself an expensive gadget after complaining about your charge card bills, buy yourself an even more outrageous gift. When he flies off the handle for no apparent reason, do the same a few days later. He'll blame it on PMS, but you'll know it's really MPA—Male Passive-Aggression—at its best.

"MY PROBLEM AND HOW I SOLVED IT"

My husband wouldn't close the closet door until the dog dragged his shoes out and chewed them up.

Jane T., Lake Forest, Illinois

TRUE STORY

One day, as the man of the house strolled across white carpeting to his throne and the remote control, he spotted something on the family room floor. He bent over and picked it up, examining a tiny something between his fingers. When he figured out what it was, he dropped it back on the floor!

When questioned, he said he thought the speck was a bug, but since it was just a rubber band, he put it back.

Why didn't he just throw it away?

STUPID MEN TRICK

You can also use the dishwasher to cook food! Bake fish in the top rack by wrapping it in foil, then running the appliance as usual (socks, dishes, and all).

❧ 9 ❧

❧ Intelligence ❧

Whether or not the *Homo slobbius* has evolved intelligence depends on whether you're talking to a man or a woman. Let's explore the development of male intelligence by examining topics ranging from men and common sense—a contradiction in terms?—to what makes them laugh.

Men and common sense

Quiz time. Read 1 through 5 carefully, then decide whether the behavior described is that of a man or a woman. Remember that truth is stranger than fiction, and these things really happened.

1. The headlight on your long, old car blows out. It's raining, so you put the car in the garage to change the light. Because you back the car into the garage, the front end sticks out onto the driveway. You change the headlight in the rain.

2. You discover liquid soap. At baby's bath time, you squirt it all over the little dear, swish her around in the tub a few times, then pull her out without scrubbing or rinsing her.

3. You load the dishwasher with the glasses straight up so that the water can collect in them.

4. As the leader of a preschool exercise class, you introduce the children to a game they love. In a room with no windows, you turn off the lights so it's pitch black and yell, "Run around as hard and fast as you can!"

5. You apply makeup while driving a car.

Answers: Give yourself 10 points for each of these correct answers: (1) man, (2) man, (3) man, (4) man, (5) woman.

Scoring: *50:* Nice work, ma'am. *40:* Okay, so maybe you don't put makeup on in the car. *20–30:* Study for the next quiz. Ask your husband to do the dishes or give the baby a bath. *10:* Your mascara needs a touch-up. *0:* Hey, pal—this is a woman's book! Get back to the sports section!

There is a rumor—circulating among those who would score highly on this quiz—that some men are a little weak in the common sense department.

Webster's New World Dictionary defines "common sense" as "ordinary good sense or sound practical judgment—usually a skill associated with females." (I made up that last part.) My working definition is based on something my mother says when she encounters an individual lacking common sense: *"How can anyone so smart be so stupid???"*

Ned Herrmann, a North Carolina consultant who helps businesses understand how people think, believes there's something to my mother's question. "Some people are absolutely dense when it comes to their thinking ability. . . . They could be very intelligent, but almost devoid of any sensible capabilities in any other areas," he notes. This is a Ph.D.'s way of saying some people are book-smart but life-stupid. Herrmann believes this happens when we invest too much of our time in subjects we're interested in, and completely avoid others. This lack of interest in particular activities (housework) leads to an overdevelopment in other areas (golf).

Robert Butterworth, Ph.D., a clinical psychologist practicing in the Los Angeles area, views common sense as "conventional wisdom," and whether you have it depends on how you were brought up and your current role. For example, a woman thinks that it's "only common sense" to clean up a puddle on the floor. But a man will walk over it, around it, or through it—waiting for it to evaporate, perhaps—rather than clean it up because he's been raised to believe cleaning is a woman's task.

Neil Chethik, author of the syndicated newspaper column *VoiceMale,* also sees social forces at work. "Women have more common sense when it comes to raising children because little girls learn these things from their mothers, while little boys are playing sports and games," he says. This is because boys need to use those grunting sounds learned on the football field to communicate on the telephone later, as adults.

Radu Bogdan, a philosophy professor at Tulane University, notes, "Many of the capabilities of men and women develop differently because of what the environment asks of them. Women see patterns and implications because they've had to pay attention to protect their young and to perform other tasks." This explains why *I* instruct my children to always, *always* stay away from cars by walking on the sidewalk, while a neighbor father uses the middle of the street to teach his toddler son how to walk.

Chethik thinks men have more common sense than women when it comes to business relationships and knowing how to fix things. "I know very successful and competent professional women who don't ask for a raise when offered a new job. A man knows that, even if he doesn't deserve the raise, he should ask for it because it suggests the man thinks he's worth more money." (While this might suggest *chutzpah* more than common sense, it does say something about male attitudes on the job.)

Bogdan views common sense a little differently, noting it's "a manner of judging people and situations." He has observed situations where women on a committee have brought common sense to a particular issue through judgment that is more balanced than that of men in the group.

Both Chethik and Bogdan see changes on the horizon as traditional sex roles evolve. "I'd like to study today's young career women in thirty or forty years," philosopher Bogdan says, "to see if they suffer from that 'mild absentmindedness' we see in men who are away from the home all day."

Now *that* would be an interesting change.

"MY PROBLEM AND HOW I SOLVED IT"

One morning my husband and I had a terrible fight over how we should discipline our children. We couldn't agree, and I left the house for work feeling as if my opinions and suggestions had been completely discounted without a second thought.

Because of the argument, I didn't have time to pack a lunch, so I stopped at the supermarket on the way to work. As I passed the floral department, I had a great idea. I ordered a dozen long-stemmed red roses and had them delivered to my home with a note. It said, "Sometimes I forget that we're on the same side. Love, Your Husband."

It took three days but we finally worked it out, and he laughed about the flowers, even though he paid for them.

I smiled and said that, the next time, I might find my way to the jewelry store.

Paula L., Colorado Springs, Colorado

TRUE STORY

During a recent physical, an intern took over when the female patient's physician left to take a call. He asked her about her medical history, working from head to toe. When she was done, he said, 'Why haven't you told me about your abdominal surgery?'

"What abdominal surgery?" she replied.

"The one that caused this scar!" he exclaimed, pointing to a thin line running straight down from her belly button.

"Well, that would be from my pantyhose," she explained nicely. He left the room immediately without saying a word, and she never saw him again.

STUPID MEN TRICK

To clean your children's faces, use the same washcloth you just used to wipe up a spill on the floor. But don't rinse it first.

Men who can do more than one thing at a time

There are none.

Adult education for men

We'd like to see these courses added to the curriculums of adult education programs nationwide.

1. You Can Do Housework Too
2. PMS—Learning When to Keep Your Mouth Shut
3. How to Fill an Ice Tray
4. We Do Not Want Sleazy Underwear for Christmas
5. Understanding the Female Response to Your Coming In Drunk at 4 A.M.
6. Effective Laundry Techniques (formerly titled: "Don't Wash My Silk Blouse")
7. Parenting Does Not End with Conception
8. Learn to Cook
9. How Not to Act Like a Jerk When You Are Obviously Wrong
10. Understanding Your Financial Incompetence
11. Reasons to Give Flowers
12. How to Stay Awake After Sex
13. Why It Is Unacceptable to Relieve Yourself Anywhere but in the Bathroom
14. Garbage—Getting It to the Curb
15. Sexual Needs 101—You Can Fall Asleep Without It If You Really Try
16. Sexual Needs 112—"The Morning Dilemma"—If It's Awake, Take a Shower
17. I'll Wear It If I Damn Well Please
18. How to Put the Toilet Seat Down
19. "The Weekend" and "Sports" Are Not Synonyms
20. Give Me a Break—How We Know Your Excuses Are Just Excuses
21. How to Go Shopping with Your Mate Without Getting Lost
22. The Remote Control—Overcoming Your Dependency
23. "Romance" and "Sex" Aren't Synonyms
24. Helpful Postural Hints for Couch Potatoes

25. Mothers-in-Law Are People Too

26. How Not to Act Younger than Your Children

27. You, Too, Can Be a Designated Driver

28. Leaving Your Friends at Home When You Take Your Wife Out

29. Honest, You Don't Look Like Mel Gibson—Especially When Naked

30. Changing Your Underwear—It Really Works

31. The Attainable Goal—Omitting "!%@%" from Your Vocabulary

32. Fluffing the Blankets After Farting Is Not Necessary

Nyuk, nyuk, nyuk! Men explain their attraction to the Three Stooges

Try this experiment: At a party, say to a man—any man—"Pick two!" Then *almost* poke him in the eyes with two fingers. He will react in typical Curly fashion, bouncing off another guy, who will do something Moe-like to a Larry, and on it goes, like dominoes tumbling.

Nyuk, nyuk, nyuk!

Men love the Three Stooges. Women don't.

"Men laugh at them while women flinch," observes Peter Sinclair, editor of *King, Warrior, Magician, Weenie: Contemporary Men's Humor.*

"When I'm watching them and a woman walks in, she rolls her eyes and says, 'When is this guy going to grow up?' I wonder about that myself sometimes," admits Dave Manzi, a devotee in Boxford, Massachusetts, who watches the trio whenever they're on TV.

Paul Williams, an air traffic controller from Frederick, Maryland, knows it's a guy thing because of the responses he gets to the Stooges messages on answering machines for two phone lines in his house. "I can always tell if it's a guy calling because he's laughing so hard he can't talk. Women speak immediately, usually saying something like, 'Oh, that's just so stupid!' " he notes.

Williams's machine messages are very Stooge-like and should

be—he and a brother spent eight hours tearing the kitchen apart banging pan lids with frying pans to perfect the metallic sounds of Moe's encounter with Curly's head. In addition to the perfect sound effects, the messages include the classic singing "Hello, hello, hello!," "Oh, a wise guy!," and appropriate Stooge language, including "moron" and "numskull."

Why would a grown man go to so much trouble to make the Three Stooges an integral part of his life? "It appeals to my sense of silliness," explains Dave DuFour, an Elkhart, Indiana, entertainer. "There have been times when I've had a boss or two dumb enough to fall for 'pick two,' " he confesses.

Sinclair believes it is part psychological, part genetic. "Men are not allowed to express their emotions, feel empathetic pain, or express their own pain. Therefore, great catharsis comes when somebody gets their nose pinched or their head bonked," he explains. "I also think it's hardwired," he hastens to add. "Guys are much more able to appreciate physical humor and much more willing to laugh at things that cause pain."

Izzy Gesell, a nationally known speaker and writer on the role of humor in our lives, says that's because men are brought up to associate physical contact with fun. "Boys are not trained to feel comfortable expressing emotions verbally. They express their emotions physically, by horsing around and playing. They relate to that when they see the physical humor of the Three Stooges," he says. Gesell also notes that, typically, men relate to the aggressor in the joke, and women relate to the victim, so Stooge humor in particular, with the pain inflicted on the victims, makes some women uncomfortable.

Sinclair believes the humor of the Stooges represents part of what makes a man a man. "When men get together in groups, you'll see that kind of painful play. If you don't go along with it, you're not in the club—you're not one of the guys," he notes.

"Nobody gets hurt, really," adds DuFour. "Part of what makes the Stooges funny is that they are live human beings appearing to hurt each other in ways only cartoon characters can." The effect is also similar to contemporary violent movies, Sinclair notes. "When Moe twists Larry's nose with a wrench, or Schwarzenegger runs through a hail of bullets without getting hit, then causes an incredible explosion, it's a form of exaggeration that's humorous."

Manzi, an engineer, makes a similar comparison. "It's a release—it's so mindless, like watching a Schwarzenegger movie. It's a break from reality."

"It's violence without the gore," agrees air traffic controller Williams.

Williams and DuFour say the "complete stupidity of it" makes them laugh. "Their movies contain an element of predictability, too—the characters are endlessly optimistic. Those morons head right into it," Williams says, and laughs.

The Stooges generate belly laughs because they are clowns without makeup, offering sight gags and sound effects that are irresistible. So if you want to date a man with a sense of humor, hang around the Three Stooges section of the videotape store. You're likely to find a guy who knows how to laugh.

"MY PROBLEM AND HOW I SOLVED IT"

There are times when I really want to see a particular movie and my husband wants to see something else. When this happens, we've learned that sometimes the best solution is to go to the theater together, but purchase tickets for different shows. He goes into one room at 7 P.M., I enter another at the same time, and we meet again in the lobby when the movies are over. He gets his share of action adventure and I've enjoyed a romantic comedy. Then we go out for a snack and talk about what we liked in the different movies we watched.

Toni W., Wheeling, Illinois

TRUE STORY

While visiting a friend, a woman commented on the unusual red and blue pattern adorning the top of a metal toaster oven. Her friend explained that the decorator touch came from melted plastic—her husband likes to use the toaster oven without removing whatever sits on top of it—usually a loaf of bread in a plastic bag.

STUPID MEN TRICK

Use the microwave oven to dry your laundry. The trick is to flip the garment every ten seconds.

ADD in adult males:
Arrested Development Disorder

Your husband grips your hand as the doctor enters the room with the test results. The doctor's expression is grim. "I'm sorry, but at least there's no doubt," he begins. "John suffers from ADD in adult males."

You gasp, horrified. "Why, ADD! Isn't that"—you shudder—"Arrested Development Disorder?"

"Yes," the doctor replies. "But if you both work together, it can be cured. John can't beat this alone," he cautions.

John sits numbly, barely believing what he's just heard. "I thought ADD was just the problem of guys who seem stuck in junior high—guys who say, 'I know you are, but what am I?' when they're angry—things like that. . . ." he mumbles, his voice tapering off.

"Yes, that's true," the doctor says consolingly. "Why, I once diagnosed a man who wore an official NBA uniform and had a life-size cutout of Michael Jordan next to the TV when he watched the Chicago Bulls. But that's an extreme case. In most men, ADD is much subtler than that."

In many men, Arrested Development Disorder is characterized by an inability or unwillingness to share feelings or preferences with another, according to David Olson, Ph.D., a psychologist in the Family Social Science Department at the University of Minnesota in St. Paul.

"It's very common," he says. Classic examples are men who say, "I don't care, you decide," or "I don't know." "They *do* care, and they *do* have a preference—they just don't want to put the energy into thinking about it," Olson explains. "They are afraid or lazy, or have gotten away without expressing opinions in the past."

Norman Pointer, M.D., a psychiatrist in private practice in Fairport, New York, says another example is the man who wants to be mothered. "He wants his woman to be nice and solicitous, to lay out his clothes for him, to praise him continually," Pointer explains.

Barry Duncan, Ph.D., director of the Dayton Institute for Family Therapy and co-author of *Overcoming Relationship Impasses,* explains the problem succinctly: "Most men are socially retarded," he says. "They don't pick up social clues the way women do."

The cause of ADD in adult males is simple, or complicated, depending on whom you talk to. Psychologist Olson says it's the result of a lack of life experiences, inability to learn from the social environment, or "inadequate training by females."

Pointer, the psychiatrist, says it comes from a childhood wound. "The natural response to a wound is to try to heal it," he explains. In other words, the adult male with arrested development could be reacting to either too much—or too little—of something in his childhood. For example, the man who refuses to accept responsibility at home might have had too much responsibility forced on him when he was young, or perhaps he had no responsibilities at all and consequently has not learned to accept any as an adult.

"Pshaw," says Howard Markman, Ph.D., a psychologist and co-author of *We Can Work It Out: Making Sense of Marital Conflict.* He thinks ADD is a "dangerous, harmful, and blaming term," and says that, unlike his peers, he doesn't believe in the concept. "The man who seems selfish or doesn't care about the thoughts or reactions of others is, in fact, very withdrawn in the relationship, and that's why he comes across as if he only cares about himself," Markman asserts.

Or maybe he's a jerk.

But Markman suggests the woman involved with such a man "look at what's going on in the relationship."

Duncan offers more concrete help. "Try indirect means of influence. Pay him back with negative consequences."

Duncan cites the case of a client who had tried for years to get her husband to help with the laundry. "Her solution was to serve him raw meatloaf for dinner, then apologize profusely and accept complete blame. She explained that she was just so busy her mind wasn't on cooking dinner the way it should be. She did this regularly until her husband was confused enough to reorganize his thinking.

"He thought about what was going on in her life that distracted her from preparing a proper meal for him and realized that, if he helped out more, maybe she'd have less to do and could focus on dinner. He started doing the laundry without her doing any nagging," Duncan reports.

"The best part about this 'payback' approach is that you feel good because you've discharged some anger while you actually get results," he adds.

Pointer suggests examining *your* role in the behavior, too. "It takes two to tango," he reminds us. "Women allow men to do this."

And, Pointer warns, if you decide to change how you relate to this behavior, "Be prepared for the repercussions." If you decide you will no longer praise and admire your companion for every little accomplishment, as you would a "wonderful little boy," expect that little boy to rebel. He might decide he doesn't want to play with someone who doesn't fawn over his every deed.

Psychologist Olson notes, however, that if you don't work to obtain the changes you need in the relationship, you'll eventually be frustrated enough to leave him anyway.

With the relationship at risk, though, it might be safer to take the advice of Confucius, who once told the young women of his village, "If you can't beat 'em, join 'em." Leave your dirty laundry on the floor, demand praise for clipping your toenails, and put those pictures of Herman's Hermits and the Monkees back up on your bedroom wall.

Junior high *was* kind of fun, wasn't it?

"MY PROBLEM AND HOW I SOLVED IT"

I've always wondered how my husband the executive manages such incredibly complicated projects at work because he can't plan his way out of a paper bag at home.

I work evenings, and he makes frequent phone calls to my business to ask how to do this, that, or the other thing with the children. (Packing for a weekend trip generates an unusual number of inquiries.) But one day he surprised me by not only assuming responsibility for fixing a problem at home, but handling it without calling me even once. When I got home, I complimented him on his success, but had to ask how he'd managed to accomplish so much without following his usual telephone routine.

"Honey," he informed me in the most serious way, "I just pretended I was at work."

Rhonda S., Tulsa, Oklahoma

True Story

A boyfriend asked to keep his dog in his girlfriend's backyard temporarily. She said he could as long as he cleaned up the mess. To clean the yard, he wore huge gloves and used a long shovel and big garbage bag. He looked like a nuclear power plant worker.

He was almost done when she pointed out a pile he'd missed. He said he'd seen it, but it was a cat pile, not a dog pile. The cat that made that mess must have been a mountain lion! She doesn't know how he could distinguish a cat pile from a dog pile, or why he even needed to. But the cat pile stayed there.

Stupid Men Trick

One fellow vacuums his head with his Shop-Vac after every haircut.

✦ 10 ✦

Is Evolution
❧ Possible? ❧

∾∾

If there's a predominant theme in the information offered by male experts in this book, it's that much of who a man is today can be blamed on that wacky male hunter of yesteryear, the caveman. The needs of the caveman supposedly explain everything from why older men date significantly younger women, to why men don't like to ask for directions when lost.

Do these people think we docile female gatherers are idiots? Are women honestly expected to believe that we are dumped by our male companions as we age because they are subconsciously seeking "cues to youth"—indications of fertility—in women with clear, unwrinkled skin?

We're told, too, that a good sense of direction was crucial to the survival of early man because one wrong turn could lead him so far from food that he would perish. If that is true, then the survivors who went on to procreate their species would have a good sense of direction and rarely get lost—and their offspring would be the same way. So how does that account for the preponderance of men who get lost on the highway, then torture us by refusing to ask for directions?

Another prevailing school of thought, particularly among psychologists, is that accepting that men are inherently different from women lets men off the hook. One male psychologist, who declined to be interviewed for this book because he prefers to focus on the similarities among men and women, told me, "That's like saying, 'He can't help it, he's a man!' You can't do that. You have to expect more of him." What this psychologist does not understand is that the "he can't help it, he's a man" theory is what helps keep many of us from enrolling in a Lorena Bobbitt Seminar for Stress Management. There are occasions when the only consolation is to say we can expect nothing better.

Others believe gender differences make life interesting. (That's a euphemism if I've ever heard one.) In a recent conversation, an otherwise intelligent man told me he was confused by this book's title. "Why not *celebrate* the differences?" he asked. I replied, "You're kidding, right?"

Really! Is he asking us to have a party to honor the male tendency to appear so incompetent at home that we will never again ask our mate to do laundry, bathe the baby, or change bed sheets? Should we build a monument to the man who rolls up his car windows, locks them with his electric controls, then passes gas to the point where his sister gags in the passenger seat? Do we develop an elaborate ritual to honor the adult male who reaches age forty without progressing from junior high to adulthood? Are these special occasions catered, or can we just tie on our aprons and serve beer, cereal, and pizza—the foods men serve themselves when left on their own?

Of course, there are some differences worth celebrating. If I were to encourage a monument to manliness, I would ask that it pay tribute to bravery, physical strength, an ability to stay calm, and a respect for straightforward communication. Many of us get our emotional strength from our men—fathers, friends, husbands, neighbors—who set a fine example, especially in a crisis.

Sometimes this is enough. Yet too often it isn't, as women reach for more in life, expecting better things for themselves and from their companions. Surrounded and influenced by different types of lifestyles and relationships, we are in a very confusing and transitional period for both women *and* men. In my own little world, I see such extremes: At one end of the spectrum, a thirty-year-old woman who orders food her husband likes when she dines out—so he'll enjoy her leftovers the next day; at the other end, women who struggle to retain their identities after marriage. I see women who expect very little from their male companions in terms of help with the home or children, and I have met men who stay home to be full-time parents, recognizing that their wives are more interested in pursuing careers.

Some of us see a smattering of hope—maybe we meet a man who changes a lightbulb within forty-eight hours instead of two weeks—and we get frustrated, wondering why our own partner can't meet more of our expectations. We forget that the grass isn't always greener on the other side of the fence.

To paraphrase Erma Bombeck, the reality is that the grass is usually greener over the septic tank, meaning, the guy who seems to be a little more evolved in one area is probably a complete Neanderthal with something else. It's much like the universal female debate: "What's worse, a man who refuses to do anything around the house, or the man who insists on making all major repairs himself—then screws them up and you have to pay a repairman twice as much to straighten out the mess?" Like "Which came first, the chicken or the egg?," it's a question with no answer.

That's not to say that the situation cannot change. But it will take time. If there is to be less stress and strain between *Homo sapiens* and *Homo slobbius,* men and women both will have to change how they view the world and each other. This evolutionary—and revolutionary, for that matter—process begins with our children. We must teach them that there is no such thing as "men's work" or "women's work." We need to stop encouraging our little boys to "act like a man" when "acting like a man" cuts them off from how they *feel.* We have to show our daughters how to be more direct when they speak—"I'm thirsty!" isn't the same as "Please get me a drink." We must be more conscious of how we relate to babies—studies prove that people treat boy babies differently from girl babies—because the ways in which we relate differently to boys and girls helps contribute to unnecessary gender differences.

Women who want and need their male companions to change

have to expect more from them. And we have to make those expectations known. Likewise, women who are happy with their 1950s lifestyle need not do anything to change it.

A few tips for men who want to stimulate change:

- Explore the world outside work so you identify less with your job.
- Wear pink shirts occasionally.
- Volunteer (not a word currently in the male vocabulary) for more tasks at work and at home that are not traditionally viewed as "male."
- Reduce your gas output.
- Don't be paranoid about whether or not your son seems "effeminate." There are worse things in life than having a female outlook.
- Don't treat your female companion like a built-in maid.

Advice for women who feel they cannot survive without change:

- When you ask for a man's help, let him do it *his* way, even though it's not how you would do it. At least it's getting done.
- Don't try to create too much change too quickly.
- Secure more free time for yourself by learning the male method of avoiding responsibility: feign incompetence.
- Increase your gas output.
- Lower your standards at home—the world won't end if you leave dirty dishes in the sink for a few days or if you have to rewash a load of clothes because mildew set in while the stuff sat in the washer for three days.
- Raise your expectations of men—they are actually capable of initiating productive behavior.
- Remove all kitchen knives from the home.

In my ideal world, men would be a little more like women, and women would be a little more like men. In that world, the empty roll of toilet paper *will actually be replaced by a man,* and the woman won't complain about whether the paper hangs from the back of the roll or from the front of it.

Why Can't a Man Be More Like a Woman? was inspired by the award-winning newsletter *The Do(o)little Report.* To subscribe to the newsletter, call 1-800-836-4467 for credit card orders or send $15.95 to *The Do(o)little Report,* P.O. Box 1121, Fairport, NY 14450.